Ministries Administrative Assurance Plan (MAAP)

Dr. V. L. Ball

WESTBOW® PRESS
A DIVISION OF THOMAS NELSON & ZONDERVAN

WestBow Press books may be ordered through booksellers or by contacting:

WestBow Press
A Division of Thomas Nelson & Zondervan
1663 Liberty Drive
Bloomington, IN 47403
www.westbowpress.com
1 (866) 928-1240

ISBN: 978-1-4908-4398-8 (sc)
ISBN: 978-1-4908-4399-5 (hc)
ISBN: 978-1-4908-4397-1 (e)

Library of Congress Control Number: 2014912193

Printed in the United States of America.

WestBow Press rev. date: 7/23/2014

FOREWARD

Verna Ball's Ministries Administrative Assurance Plan is a priceless literary work that will stand the test of time. It will prove to transcend generations. It is a jewel that paints the principles of leadership and administration with the brush of pragmatic application for Kingdom advancement. Practically every paragraph is stocked with concepts that makes one consider his approach to ministry. The author takes the abstract and makes it plain that all may comprehend the principles of ministry development. The use of real life analogies and the explanation of original word usages will empower all to understand and even communicate the concepts of this work. This is a wonderful blend of theological mandates being married to corporate strategies to give birth to kingdom effectiveness.

This book provides a mirror to discern areas of concern and immediately supplies the solutions for the shortcomings. It is replete with strategies and language that may be applied to any ministry setting. The author takes the reader from definition to application and implementation. The book flows in a natural sequential order that is easy to digest and retain. It will focus the reader on the intangible factors of successful leadership in ministry. This book will make a distinct difference in the understanding of any leader on any level.

R.C. Blakes, Jr.

FOREWARD

Unequivocally, without a doubt, naturally the administrative support system is important to the foundational structure of any church. It assist in varies areas to allow the vision to flow without catastrophic hindrances. The administrative department handles the majority if not all of the business dealings to any church. I am one that believes that the Church is not a business but we as the people of God must do business. When we have the proper foundational tools to build our ministries on we can function in the fullness of our potential. The bible declares that we are many members but one body (1 Corinthians 12:12), and when the people chosen to handle the Administrative duties work as a team with the leader in varies areas it moves to the perfecting of the God given vision.

We believe in Jesus and that he is the way but God gives man vision and knowledge about what he wants completed but it is up to us to obtain that knowledge and not destroy what has been put in our hands. ("..my people are destroyed for the lack of knowledge.." Hosea 4:6). There are natural abilities, wisdom and experiences that are needed so that the Body of Christ can make the impact needed across the world. Operating with a Kingdom mentality goes beyond what we once thought. It requires structure, unity, discipline, leadership, and so much more.

Dr. Verna L. Ball consistently throughout this book makes the necessary process clear in how we can affectively transcend our churches to meet astronomical results as some build and others expand in that which God ordained. As you embark on this journey you will understand that God is using her in this latter day to assist his people to be more structured in not only the things of God but in the land in which we live in. Consecration, wisdom, spiritual knowledge, experience, and insight on a corporeal level went in to the construction of this plan. The information and strategic steps that you will see can be astonishingly rewarding only if implemented.

This is important to the pastor just starting his church or organization in how to set up and do business of the church. This relives a lot of pressure and allows focus on spiritual things of God, your vision and what God is giving. Even after 30 years of pastoring, I have been able to glean from the material because as we expand as a seasoned ministry there are intricate details that are needed to set up and prepare for next level ministry.

I believe in not only this author but also in what God has ordained her to do. Our obedience to the things of God and the application of the knowledge shared in this book will result with us as the Body of Christ being strengthened, and see a shift in every area of our ministries.

~Apostle Garfield Curlin, Th. D
All Nations House Of Prayer
Hopkinsville, KY

DEDICATION

To my astoundingly loving family pops, mother, daughter, and my remarkable, sweet little granddaughter, Taylor, the apple of my eye, thank you for your unending loving support, listening ears, faith-filled prayers, and the family kitchen gatherings with New Orleans-style coffee *where you can smell and taste the love*!

Thank you to my extended family and brothers in the Gospel Dr. Dennis D. Winborn and Dr. Anthony Flaniken, mighty men of God who are strong in the Lord. Thank you for your listening ear, insightful talks, and the richness and the depth in the exchanges of the Word of God. s'agapo (Σ>αγαπώ) with the love of the Lord. I am deeply privileged to call you friends.

To each of my instructors, especially, my teacher and mentor gone home, I am deeply thankful to God for all that was shared with me. You stretched me and made a deposit within me for which I will always be grateful.

To Mrs. Hollie Roberts, I am profoundly thankful for your time, wisdom, and kindness in reviewing this work. It is a pleasure to know such a virtuous and gifted godly woman.

To my father in the Gospel, Bishop Robert C. Blakes, Jr. you are a remarkable visionary, impactful leader, profoundly anointed teacher, an example of a godly family man and a loving pastor. Thank you for your support, encouragement, and guidance. The Lord has been gracious to me with the privilege and high honor to be a true daughter. I thank God for New Home Ministries.

With my deepest gratitude to my friend, brother, and apostle the Lord delighted to send into my life; thank you apostle Garfield Curlin, ThD for your support; you are a giant among apostles. Not only are you a noteworthy visionary, you are a great leader of great men and women. For such a mighty apostle, we are indeed thankful for your humble spirit that continuously points us to Christ. The Lord almighty has been overwhelmingly good to me in bringing you into my life. Those of us who are privileged to be connected to you know the value of your wisdom, godliness, and deep understanding of the Word and the Spirit of God.

To my friend for over 30 years and brother in the Gospel, apostle Eugene Satterwhite, ThD, DD, you have seen me in the best of times and the worst of times. And, through it all we have remained the best of friends. You are an amazing author and walking Bible, a legend in your own lifetime. So, many of us stand amazed that a man with so many gifts can be so humble in spirit. From you we learn what true godliness looks like. It is no surprise that you and apostle Curlin were named the brothers of thunder.

And, a very special Thank You to Westbow Press for believing in my work enough to take on this, my first project.

Addressed lastly, but You are first in my life and above all others.
Thank You my God for this work, for your graciousness, blessings,
and continual favor upon my life. In the words of a song, written
by a great theologian gone home, Dr. Barbara Wright,
"I Stand Amazed"!
I am honored to dedicate my first book to all of you.

CONTENTS

INTRODUCTION

Welcome to the Ministries Administrative Assurance Plan. This book was written to assist ministries in developing administrative programs that deliver time and time again. Through the integration of genuine leadership, biblical principles, and modern administrative practices, MAAP will aid in ensuring your assignment is accomplished. Wealth often begins with an idea, but for conceptualization that idea must then be written, organized, resourced, and set in motion. The believer's task is to build God's kingdom while here on earth. As believers, we are commanded to increase. It is this increase that gives us the ability to advance the kingdom of God. Since advancing takes money, assets, and resources, it is essential for every born-again believer to implement the gifts and the ideas the Lord has spoken into his or her life. The kingdom of God is not financed by paupers, thus every born-again believer is under assignment to prosper to bring forth his purpose for our lives. If we accept the will of God as our will, then our purposes will be in harmony with his. As leaders, we have a responsibility to distribute the wealth gained in accord with God's plan, and he will continuously supply and establish us in order to maintain our functional position on the frontline of contributing to his kingdom agenda.

A time ago, some folks whom I still call friends deemed me inconsequential to the effort of financing the kingdom based on my physical appearance. At the time, I did not quite know how to engage them as I grappled with the thought that they might be right. For me, the idea of not being able to produce, not being able to make a difference, was too much to handle at the time. Interestingly, once my focus was realigned, the answer to my dilemma, which had been blotted out by my overwhelming needs, was glaring me in the face. "Promotion cometh neither from the east, nor from the west, nor from the south. But God is the judge: he putteth down one, and setteth up another" (Psalm 75:6–7). I wanted to prosper, but it had to be on God's terms. It is he who gives us ideas, thoughts, and the creativity that delivers us.

What we do with what he has provided is entirely up to us. If we squander his blessings, let us not raise our fists to the high God. Take some time. Step back if you need to, but write the vision. If you are ever to achieve your goals, you must be bold, brave, and hungry enough to lay them out on paper. Put applicable structure to the thoughts that have been rambling around in your mind. Then, to aptly administrate the mission, it will take a written vision and people to carry it out. People are a resource that can be tasked to help to promulgate, plan, and work the mission defined by your vision.

We often know what we want to do, but how to get there is unclear. The ministry of administration is the pathway that can make the mission and the vision a reality. This is the spirit from which this work has been written. The Ministries Administrative Assurance Plan (MAAP) is designed to provide a continual resource to aid in the development of a Word-based administrative plan. The aim was to equip God's servants with a functional tool that supports the fulfillment of individual mandates and callings. Although this plan, which I have coined MAAP, was written specifically with ministries in mind, any organization can benefit from using its practical application. This work endeavors to align administrative processes and practices with God's divine order by revealing God's intent in the ministry of administrative management.

> His intention was the perfecting and the full equipping of the saints (His consecrated people), [that they should do] the work of ministering toward building up Christ's body (the church), [that it might develop] until we all attain oneness in the faith and in the comprehension of the [full and accurate (Marvin Vincent, *Word Studies*)] knowledge of the Son of God, that [we might arrive] at really mature manhood (the completeness of personality, which is nothing less than the standard height of Christ's own perfection), the measure of the stature of the fullness of the Christ and the completeness found in him.
> —Ephesians 4:12 (AB)

We will examine the interface aspects between the Bible, people, and how biblical principle pairs with practice and the implications of its effect on conditions in and outside of the church. MAAP was written to aid leaders with a godly approach to administrative ministry. It offers a systematic, tactical approach to administrative management for service to the body of Christ.

My objective has been the same since the time that I started ministry: to help prepare Christian leaders by providing sound leadership resources and by offering godly concepts that improve efficiency and effectiveness within ministry.

CHAPTER 1

The Genesis

From the times of Adam through the days of our patriarchal father, Abraham, to the local church that now exists thousands of years after the New Testament era of Christ, God has chosen significant leaders. The Lord has prepared his servants for the task of leading his people through the use of organization. Moses, a leader of God's chosen people, was born a Hebrew slave. Yet, by divine intervention, he was brought up under the leadership, guidance, and influence of pharaoh, the ruler of Egypt. This same Egypt, located on the continent of Africa, was the first world power. God chose who and what this born-slave would become before he was placed in his mother's womb. Although he fled from Egypt to escape punishment for a crime he had committed, Jehovah, who identified himself as *ehyeh asher ehyeh* (transliterated), interpreted as "I am that I am," sent him back to the place he ran from. The one true and living God sent him back as a demigod to reveal to all of Egypt that *ehyeh asher ehyeh* alone is God.

Although he had grown up with access to literature, history, calligraphy, and the like, Moses gave up his Egyptian privileges and inheritance because he identified with something greater than himself. Instead of enjoying the fruits of a fortified, well-established, rich environment, in the face of opposition he chose to make his abode on the backside of the desert on Mount Horeb. he remained in this desert place until God trained him and fully prepared him to go forth and lead the chosen people out of four hundred years of cruel bondage.

Understand that Egypt was no small prize! Egypt was a highly organized society of sophisticated systems in commerce, transportation, and structured with a powerful government. It was in Egypt that Moses had favor with pharaoh and direct access to the strength of Egypt's military, which was second to none.

Moses was taught the inner workings of Egypt's systems. He was given firsthand knowledge of its government, education, and its history. Yet, it appears that everything he learned was in preparation for a life of service to the most high God. Pharaoh must have thought that one day this son of Egypt who had grown up in its palace would return all the training he had provided in kind. Surely this adopted son of dual citizenship would remember the benevolence shown to him and would choose to become the next leader of Egypt in order to return what he had so freely received. However, Proverbs 19:21 reminds us that "Many designs are in a man's mind, but it is the Lord's plan that is accomplished" (JPS).

The apostle Paul, much like Moses, grew up with a type of dual citizenship. The apostle was Hebrew, yet he grew up as a Roman citizen. Paul was Saul of Tarsus, well known in the synagogues and popular for his great acts in persecuting Christians. His upbringing was in the capital of the Roman province of Cilicia, the home of a prestigious Roman university in the school of philosophy.

Similar to Moses, the Apostle Paul came from a highly organized culture. The Romans took much pride in their culture. They were known to revere knowledge and crafts and their skills were cunning. They embraced the Greeks, for Greece had set the bar high as a place for scholars and people of thought with its knowledge in great subjects like philosophy, science, religion, and the arts. Greeks like Aristotle and Plato, as well as many of their protégés, were of the most important philosophers of their day.

Like the Greeks, the Romans became a mighty power, who borrowed information from many other nations such as Greece, Mesopotamia, and even Egypt. As Rome conquered the known world, they continued to absorb the best of other cultures to structure themselves as "the place" for philosophy and academia. Undoubtedly, the apostle himself gained a considerable education while attending the University of Tarsus. He was a student under the study and mentorship of the legendary Gamaliel, who was one of the most important rabbis of his day.

Both Moses and the apostle Paul received undeniably supernatural calls from God to lives of leadership. Moses was called to lead the special family whom God chose, a family who found themselves trapped into four hundred years of bondage. And, to rescue them, God spoke to this man Moses, guilty of murder, through a burning bush while he was tending his father-in-law's sheep on Mount Horeb.

Earlier, Moses had fled from Egypt for killing an Egyptian who was mercilessly flogging a Hebrew slave. Yet, despite his guilt, he was greatly used to demonstrate the miraculous power and "oneness" of God. This chosen family was no stranger to floggings, to the murder of their male babies, along with a host of other cruelties that was not uncommon to them. In hopes of relief, they cried out to the one God known as Jehovah to their fore fathers. Their fathers and fathers father had passed down the knowledge and understanding of their God in stories from one generation to the next. Each generation learning to call upon Jehovah, the God of their fore-fathers, who was, is, and will always be the Self-Existent God. After four hundred years of living through ruthless and callous oppression, Jehovah was about to show up in their lives. Their God had finally come to deliver them through his servant Moses with astounding strength and incomparable miracles. The Almighty God had come to reveal himself by a name so holy that the Israelites feared to speak it or write it down.

In like manner, the apostle Paul was a murderer of a different sort. He persecuted Christians for teaching and believing in Jesus Christ as the Son of God. Still, Paul was converted by Christ while on the road to Damascus. His encounter with the Almighty God changed his life forever. First, the Lord blinded him, then converted him, and later miraculously healed him—all in accord with his plan and purpose. Not only did Paul become a Christian, Jesus changed his name from Saul to Paul and led him on renowned missionary journeys throughout Asia Minor that paved the way for the Christendom of Jews and Gentiles alike from that day to this one. His inroads in Eurasia advanced the kingdom of God, bringing salvation to cultures that had never known the one true God.

Both of these great yet imperfect men were educated and prepared for the leadership that lay ahead of them. In addition, they were ordained by God to record the instructions of the Sovereign Lord to us. Both men had vast experience to draw upon for their mission of bringing the people of God to salvation. Their sacrifice and service has left us with a wealth of historical data. Their work continues to reveal the order and the operation of God today, giving us the opportunity to gain insight into Christ, who laid an immovable foundation.

Note that in the Old Testament, Moses gave us a concise depiction of the priesthood with its sacrificial worship system, and in the New Testament the apostle Paul gave us instruction in the organization of the church and the operation of the ministry gifts for and within the body of Christ. Through these enormous leaders in the Gospel, we are given a front row, center stage view of godly administration at work.

CHAPTER 2

The Vision's Driving Force

Your greatest hindrance does not come from external sources. Resist the desire to put-off to tomorrow what you should do today. *Tactical* is a military term for planned action to reach a specific predetermined end. Being tactical requires planning; it is to be forward-thinking. Being tactically ready will allow a ministry to effectively meet the needs of people within communities, cities, states, provinces, and countries around the globe. This will take a functional administrative management team that is structurally developed and qualified. Yet, the reality is that not every ministry is at the stage where they have the necessary resources to appoint a strong administrative team. Regardless of whether a ministry has been around for years, months, weeks, days, or moments, it takes time to birth, train, and invest in people who can function like a team of oxen yoked together with one accord in the ministry. Therefore, one of the first assignments needed for any ministry is focusing on developing an integral leadership team.

There is no substitute for building a team of core persons with an attitude of inclusion. This is paramount to promoting ministry growth and mission success. The structure of the administrative unit must be well organized and act like a lubricated and freshly tuned engine if it is to stay a functionally running vehicle in its drive to attain the heights it is called to reach. People, processes, and systems are needed to yield these results. Therefore, a qualified administration must have at its foundation the four "P's" of *purpose* and *people* for *planning*" the *projects.*

Failure to prepare, neglect, or ineptness are not acceptable excuses for missing mission opportunities. Missions are a necessity as they are a commandment of God unto every believer. As his elect, we are here expressly to, "Go then and make disciples of all nations, baptizing them in the name of the Father and of, Jesus, the Son and of the Holy Spirit, teaching them to observe everything that I have commanded you, and behold, I am with you all the days (Perpetually, uniformly, an on every occasion), to the [very] close and consummation of the age. Amen (So let it be)" (Matthew 28:19–20 AB). No matter your Christian denomination, the work of the Great Commission is to be done until we all come into the unity of the faith, unto a perfect man, fitly joined together. Thus, the church has an obligation to organize its affairs into productivity.

If Christendom is not to be derelict in its duty to the community, the environment, and the nations at large, then it must be serviceable in the world even though it is not of it. The approach must be of sound judgment, showing prudence and an ability to handle business affairs. A major requirement of achieving this end is a mission statement. The mission statement helps oppose useless activities like impulsive buying and sinking into the quicksand of overwhelming debt, and things that contribute to the waste of resources. This behavior is called whimsical decision making, and it erodes the ministry by eating away at its resources and plunging it into desperation and danger.

Effectively managing God's ministry requires deliberate biblical attention. Meaningful biblical examination produces clarity in purpose and aids in writing a clearly focused mission statement that steers the people of God toward its assignment. It can readily be seen that an administrative plan is useful. Having a plan helps to eliminate mistakes that damage credibility and prevent premature errors that can hinder and even abort the ministry's mission.

One of my favorite television shows was an old spy drama called *Mission Impossible*. James Phelps (played by Peter Graves) would give Barney Collier (played by Greg Morris) an assignment so they could determine who or what was threatening national security. Sometimes Barney had to give the team vision that they might not otherwise have had. Barney paired vision with the team's mission to pave the way for James to carry out his assignments, which had to be completed regardless of the obstacles he might face. Herein can be seen a noteworthy division between the mission and the vision; notice that these two terms are neither synonymous nor interchangeable.

In relation to the scenario given above, one can readily see a clear distinction between these two important terms—*mission* and *vision*. When the mission and the vision work together, they form a cohesiveness that allows precision in the mission. Barney gave them the vision so they could work the mission. So, we find that if a ministry is to fulfill its mission, the leader must have written a clear vision. And a skilled team knows the necessity of having a firm grasp on both of these concepts.

Each officer must be more than familiar with the ministry's mission and its vision statements. The Mission Impossible team was highly skilled. Being well trained in their craft, they were ready to go on assignment. Let me make an important point here: not only did the Mission Impossible team keep abreast of their mission, neither the newer nor older members of the team went on a mission they were not fully committed to. They did not require cue cards or pocket guides, they fully knew their assignment.

To stay on top, training cannot be overlooked, skipped, or put aside. The well trained Mission Impossible team knew their trade exceptionally well, which should remind us that training must come first. Training is an essential element that can provide unparalleled results. Each team member should not only be taught to unmistakably know the mission but to strictly adhere to the assignment with total and complete acceptance. In so doing, the qualities of the ministry will be distinct and easily recognizable. The mission statement substantiates the vision and provides the groundwork that everyone is to follow. It is the guide or the blueprint for the success of the ministry.

Ministries without a vision are doomed to fail. Why? The vision statement gives credence to the mission. The mission statement identifies who the ministry endeavors to reach and tells what the vision is all about. More simply put, the mission statement not only identifies demographics, revealing *who* it is that the ministry is called to reach, it also instills *purpose* within the members. This sense of purpose identifies what the ministry is trying to accomplish. In short, it tells *why* God called the ministry into being. Scripture says, "And God placed all things under his feet and appointed him to be head over everything for the church, which is his body, the fullness of him who fills everything in every way" (Ephesians 1:22–23). The church is his body, and as his body our efforts should reflect service *by, to,* and *for* him. As with all things of him, the mission statement must glorify God. It should be about his work. In other words, the mission statement details the rationale while the vision precisely describes the way or the direction that the ministry is taking. Said another way, it is the roadmap because it specifically pinpoints a precise view telling *who, how, why,* and *what* of the mission. Although the how, why, and what are important, the Lord is more concerned with the who. Leaders are often ambitious and can become intently occupied and even caught up with the how, why, and the what of the things they are going to do. But without the who that Jesus wants us to reach the rest really does not matter.

In Genesis 12, God called Abram out of Haran.

> Now the Lord had said unto Abram, Get thee out of thy country, and from thy kindred, and from thy father's house, unto a land that I will show thee: And I will make of thee a great nation, and I will bless thee, and make thy name great; and thou shalt be a blessing: And I will bless them that bless thee, and curse him that curseth thee: and in thee shall all families of the earth be blessed. So Abram departed, as the Lord had spoken unto him; and Lot went with him: and Abram was seventy and five years old when he departed out of Haran.
>
> —Genesis 12:1–4

The Lord commanded Abram to leave his father's house without instructing him where to go. This lack of information did not deter Abram from obeying. The Bible says, "And Abram took Sarai his wife, and Lot, his brother's son, and all their substance that they had gathered, and the souls that they had gotten in Haran; and they went forth to go into the land of Canaan; and into the land of Canaan they came" (Genesis 12:5). In other words, Abram accepted the mission of God without asking him how he was going to complete the mission.

Abram was from Ur, Chaldea, which was a polytheistic country. They were not accustomed to serving the one true God. Yet, when the Lord called him, strikingly, he trusted him without hesitation and accepted the mission to go before even knowing the vision. God did not leave him blind, though. He taught him the mission and revealed the vision to him.

Let's backtrack: Abram stepped out of his comfort zone and into the mission in faith, believing God. In this sense, the mission behaved as a verb. It was the action that Abram implemented when he left Haran and acted on what God said by moving out in faith. Thus, the mission of a believer is to follow Christ and be like him. Therefore, an important goal of the church should be to develop followers of Christ and to teach believers to be like Jesus. There is only one way to accomplish this task: through the Word of God. First, one must recognize that self is a destroyer of grace.

Like Abram, God's mission is to train believers, teaching them to guard against self so they learn not to compromise the truth. In the time of famine, the Lord did not send Abram into Egypt, Abram went against God's will. He eventually got back on track and God prospered him greatly.

Scripture lets us know that God has provided us with a foundation upon which we are to build, "According to the grace (the special endowment for my task) of God bestowed on me, like a skillful architect and master builder I laid [the] foundation, and now another [man] is careful how he builds upon it, For no other foundation can anyone lay than that which is [already] laid, which is Jesus Christ (the Messiah, the Anointed One) (1 Corinthians 3:10–11 AB). This is the solid foundation upon which every true church must be built. Essentially, the mission statement is an open declaration announcing what the ministry anticipates achieving. It provides a philosophical view of *what* the ministry plans to accomplish based upon the strategy or the intent of the vision. In order for either to succeed, leaders are necessary.

Ephesians defines the role or the occupations of specific leaders who are gifts from God to and for the body of Christ. They are servants tasked to serve the people of God. These gifts work in set positions to edify the people of the most high God until we all come into the unity of the faith and into the knowledge of Jesus Christ. Their calling is for an explicit reason, "Until we all come unto a perfect man unto the measure of the fullness of Christ!" (Ephesians 4:13 KJV)

The significance of our role in relation to others can easily slip away from us, especially when we become relaxed, unfocused, or more concerned with our own plans, needs, and desires. It is not difficult to become preoccupied with stuff regardless of whether the stuff is important or not. Surely, church budgets, conflicts within ministry, the organizing of meetings, handling staff issues, *etc.*, all have merit. The thing to watch for is that these diversions do not cause us to lose sight or short-circuit the assignment. Issues can become a bottleneck that can distract us for longer periods of time than we expect. Although challenging, remaining focused is not only an obligation, it is a responsibility which can be fulfilling and exciting.

Struggles quite often enter through day-to-day crises. While it is important to manage each crisis, they can and often do encroach on a leader's time. An abundance of crises can easily become a hindrance that can create a type of ministry blackout that interrupts the outflow of missions.

It takes a watchful eye to prevent crises from impeding the development of new and insightful approaches to ministry. God has placed specific people within the congregation that have the skill, understanding, and willingness to address reoccurring issues in accord with the administrative plan in place. When adequately trained, they can properly handle each day-to-day crisis in a manner that suitably complies with written protocols.

Consider this analogy: no more than it is the job of a professional football player to provide himself with his own uniform is it the ministry's job to outfit itself. It is not the task of the leader to outfit the church. All leaders, regardless of the offices they hold, are gifts placed within the body of Christ by God in accord with his divine plan. In other words, outfitting the church is a job that God has established through his gifts. The gifts are to outfit the Church so that the body of Christ is equipped with the resources needed to accomplish his purpose. Achieving the mission takes a dual effort on the part of the pastor or the set leader and the appointed leadership within the ministry or organization.

Akiva Ben Joseph, a prolific Jewish scholar, regarded the Song of Solomon 7:12 as the center of the whole Bible. It serenades us with a prophetic love song about the mystery of the kingdom of God saying, "Let us rise early and go to the vineyards; Let us see whether the vine has budded and its blossoms have opened, And whether the pomegranates have bloomed. There I will give you My love" (Song of Solomon 7:12 AB).

It is the love of God that gives the momentum *that moves the heart of a leader to serve* **the needs of people. In Matthew, Jesus asked his disciple after they had finished breakfast, "Simon son of John, Do you love Me more than these?" Simon Peter answered him, "Yes, Lord; You know that I love You." Jesus then said to him, "Tend My lambs" (John 21:15). The lack within the church is not on the part of the Lord; he has fully supplied the church with all that it needs, placing gifts within**

the body to do the work of the ministry and build his church. This is accomplished through its mission and the fulfillment of its vision.

Resounding in the ear of every pastor should be, "If you love Me, tend My lambs." It is the duty of the set leader to empower others by finding new ways to proactively integrate the gifts Jesus has bestowed unto the church. In keeping with God's plan to outfit the church, these gifts are to strive to be a help in service to the pastor.

CHAPTER 3

Set the Order

In the New Testament passage of 1 Corinthians 12:28, we see *order*. In this text, the Scripture makes known not a man-made idea but a divinely orchestrated pattern, "God hath set some in the church, first apostles, secondarily prophets, thirdly teachers, after that miracles, then gifts of healings, helps, governments, diversities of tongues." Notice that God did not randomly set these gifts in the church. Rather, he was specific.

The Master identified each gift in a set order. He chose an adverb to identify *how* the thing is done. The adverb causes the reader to see within the Scripture the order that God used, "first" then "secondarily" and then "thirdly." Each adverb characterizes a particular pattern or, in other words, order.

Strong's Exhaustive Concordance of the Bible and *Vine's Expository Dictionary of Old Testament and New Testament Word*s both render the word for *administration* as *governments* or *governing*. The word *administration* comes from the Greek word *kubernesis* (κβέρνησις), which has at its root the connotation of a helmsman steering a ship. *Kubernesis* is derived from the word *kubernao*, which means *to guide* (English word used in the Bible KJV meaning *to govern*). The word denotes steering or pilotage. However, metaphorically it refers to governments or governing.

These gifts to the body, as in 1 Corinthians 12:28, are guides within the local church. The word *kubernesis* is used specifically in this text and is also the same word used in Romans 12, wherein spiritual gifts are listed. Although the Greek definition of the word identifies the helmsman as a captain, this is not always the case. The archaic meaning of the word *helm* was to cover or to furnish with a helmet. Thus, the helmsman covers, protects, or steers the head. Today, on some ships, the helmsman is the person steering the ship at the behest of the captain.

While living in Bermuda, my family and I had a little twenty-eight-foot boat. Due to my inexperience, I was only able to be the helmsman with a captain onboard. I needed to be directed by someone experienced enough to handle guiding around the coral reefs or anything else that was in the water with us, and who knew the governing laws of the authority over the waters we were in. It was necessary for me to take directions from someone more experienced and knowledgeable. Similar to my experience, the helmsman must take his cues from the captain of the ship in order to move the ship in the right direction.

The helmsman's job of steering the rudders is determined by the captain, whose job is to steer the ship. The helmsman does not take the ship wherever he wants it to go. Like me, the helmsman is to steer the ship as directed by the person in charge of the ship, the captain. And even the captain receives his directions from someone in authority over him. The captain's responsibility is to follow the mission that he or she has been given. The person giving the captain instructions on where to take the ship is the one who is responsible for strategizing the overall mission of the trip. For smooth sailing, the captain has been equipped with staff which the Scripture calls gifts (1 Cor. 12:28).

A discerning captain recognizes the importance of each position and relies on each member's obedience, skill, ability, and integrity to the mission to meet its objective. In other words, the captain must take the commanding officers on the ship into account. By consulting with the leaders in each position, we create unity and collect useful input that can help us direct the helmsmen to move the rudders in the appropriate direction.

The main objective is that the ship reaches its final destination safely by avoiding destructive collisions with the obstacles in its path. Keeping this metaphor in mind, let us now consider the church. The pastor (the captain) is responsible for leading the church and receives directional orders from God through the Holy Ghost. The Word, which is God, must always confirm in complete harmony the direction in which the pastor takes the church. The pastor then presents the direction to the leadership in order to direct the gifts (the officers) who are responsible for carrying out the mission. There is no ambiguity in the mission. The mission is clear: it is the church's objectives.

Remember, the helmsman (the appointed leader under the pastor, often the assistant pastor) is the person at the helm whose task is to steer the rudders and not the ship. As there is only one captain, there is one administration. It is made up of many bodies as there are many gifts and works, but the administration of the church is "one" under the leadership of the pastor. The responsibility of each officer resides within his or her particular area of responsibility. Each officer is to provide feedback to cohesively meet the set goal or goals of the church.

No officer directs the church! All officers take direction from the pastor to guide the church. An officer significantly impacts the church when that officer works rhythmically and harmoniously within his or her assignment. This unity and harmonious behavior among the officers serve as a great asset that allows the set leader to carry out the mission handed down by God.

The lives of the officers must be transparent; they must remain focused on their tasks. They are to provide thorough reports with all the details regarding their individual assignments to the pastor. By providing the pastor with the appropriate details of their individual tasks, the pastor can correctly administrate the church so that it operates in an orderly and cohesive manner. The Bible speaks of gifts who are active, not slothful or complacent in the body. The Scripture informs us that, "God's various gifts are handed out everywhere; but they all originate in God's Spirit. God's various expressions of power are in action everywhere; but God himself is behind it all. Each person is given something to do that shows who God is: Everyone gets in on it, everyone benefits. All kinds of things are handed out by the Spirit, and to all kinds of people! The variety is wonderful: wise counsel, clear understanding, simple trust, healing the sick, miraculous acts, proclamation, distinguishing between spirits, tongues, and interpretation of tongues. All of these gifts have a common origin, but are handed out one by one by the one Spirit of God. He decides who gets what, and when." (1 Corinthians 12:4-11 MSG) Meaning, there are various activities in operation, but it is God who is to be in control of everyone and everything within the church.

Every born-again believer has a measure of the Holy Spirit. The purpose of the Holy Spirit in the life of the believer is empowerment. This empowerment of the Holy Spirit produces spiritual wellness and wholeness within the body of Christ. For the body of Christ to be well and whole, it is important to understand and embrace the fact that we are made up of many parts. Although the statement that the body of Christ, which is made up of many, is *one* in whom Christ is the head may sound somewhat oxymoronic, it is true nonetheless. We are collectively one. Like the Borg in *Star Trek the Next Generation*, the Scripture says, "For the body is not one member but many" (1 Corinthians 12:14). There are many parts, but one body, and it is Christ who has made this body of many members.

A nugget that must not be forgotten: *he honors the member that lacks. Strong's Exhaustive Concordance of the Bible* defines this word *lacked*. It is the Greek word *hustereo* (hoos-ter-eh-o). It derives its meaning from another word that means *to be later*. It is also defined by implication to mean to be inferior or, generally, to fall short or be deficient. It can also mean to come behind or short, to be destitute, fall, lack, suffer need, (be in) want, be the worst.

We know that Christ honors the least to the greatest to prevent divisions, schisms, and isms within the body of the church. "See to it that no one carries you off as spoil or make you yourselves a captive by his so-called philosophy and intellectualism and vain deceit (fancifulness and plain nonsense), following human tradition (men's ideas of the material rather than the spiritual world), just crude notions following the rudimentary and elemental teachings of the universe and disregarding [the teachings of] Christ (The Messiah)" (Colossians 2:8 AB).

Beginning with the creation of mankind as recorded in Genesis, man has made choices that determined the type of society and culture in which he would live. Look back at man's history. There are countless accounts of intelligently orchestrated activities where he organized and strategized governments, built societies to buy and sell goods, exchanged ideas, arranged business concepts, and reared up armies. Man has used armies to enforce laws, to build systems, erect structures, and to maintain appointments of leaders whom he believed could govern over him. Regardless of all of man's plans, God has appointed leaders that he expects to labor effectively. Yet, the effectiveness of leadership must be accompanied by followers. The job of followers is to provide adequate support. Someone must lead and someone must follow.

Set the order! A clear definition of roles is critical for proper alignment to adequately run a ministry. Yet, leaders who try to do the job alone typically burn themselves out along with the followers who are there to render support. Godly leaders should be authentic so they can deliver adequate leadership and mentorship. Not only do wise leaders recognize that mentoring is a must, they also have mentors to guide them and hold them accountable. The idea of being accountable does not remove autonomy; rather, it lends to understanding that fosters respect and demonstrates responsibility. Many times the lack of visible mentorship can make suspect the authenticity of the ministry and perpetuate the idea that there is a hidden, self-serving motive, and that image can corrode respect.

Equally as important as mentoring is the practice of delegating. This element of leadership can make a resounding impact on the success of the ministry. However, it is crucial that leaders understand that delegating does not relieve them from their responsibility. Delegating is a vital part of ministry because it enables leaders to focus on the bigger picture. Herein is another reason why training is important. The act of delegating lessens the leader's distractions from those day-to-day, mundane tasks that must be done but are routine enough to be handled by trained staff. Through the useful application of delegating, leaders are able to turn their attentions to central tasks and possibly achieve "a-look-ahead" that allows them to plan forward with a keener perception.

The key to successfully delegating is structure. Getting the structure right requires applying the wisdom of the Word and following the lead of the Holy Spirit. Tasks should be assigned according to the gifts that God has bestowed.

Organizations have to grow, thus they do not always have every gift in operation in the house. It is expedient to use those obedient, willing, capable persons within the body of Christ who have invested in themselves by preparing and educating themselves to be readily available to meet the responsibilities assigned. The apostle Paul, in his letter to the church at Corinth, wrote about church conduct and how the church should govern the affairs for the body of Christ. In 1 Corinthians 14:26 (AB) he asked the question, "What then, brethren, is [the right course]? When you meet together, each one has a hymn, a teaching, a disclosure of special knowledge or information, an utterance in a [strange] tongue, or an interpretation of it. [But] let everything be constructive and edifying and for the good of all."

Our wise apostle did not leave the question unanswered for the church to come up with its own solution. Instead, he gave us the appropriate answer in 1 Corinthians 14:33 saying, "For he [Who is the source of their prophesying] is not a God of confusion and disorder but of peace and order. As [is the practice] in all the churches of the saints (God's people)" (AB). In other words, God is not a God of disorder, but Jehovah-Shalom. He is God, our peace! How, then, do we bring this peace to our ministries and our churches? The answer is Christian leadership, which must provide sound biblical instruction to the body. Without instruction, we are left with chaos.

Strong's Talking Greek Hebrew Dictionary Number 1515 defines the Greek word for *peace* as: εἰρήνη – transliterated eirēnē (phonetic pronunciation: i-ray'-nay).

> Root: probably from a primary verb eiro (to join): peace (literal or figurative); by implication *prosperity*: - one, peace, quietness, rest, + set at one again.

So, what can we glean from the apostle Paul's instructions to the church? He admonished them to confront conflicts in order to put an end to disruptions in the church, stop disorderliness, and bring order. For the church to viably serve people there must be order. The apostle cautioned the church at Corinth, "Everything must be done decently and in order." The *Message Bible* reads, "When we worship the right way, God doesn't stir us up into confusion; he brings us into harmony. This goes for all the church no exceptions." Hence, the essence here is that when we "do church" we are to do it in a good, orderly, or decent manner, which means without chaos.

The church is to be conducted sensibly with compassion and sensitivity. The body of Christ should find consistency, unity, soundness, oneness, responsibility, and such in the conduct of the church in order for it to provide proper guidance to the body. The servants of the Lord are to be ambassadors, wise stewards. As ambassadors for Christ, he expects us to administrate his work in a prudent and efficient manner.

There is no mistaking the fact that every person called by God will one day have to give an account of his or her life, including failures in obeying him. We will each stand before the Judgment Seat of God and give an account to the Almighty of all of our works. The study of the "talents" provides us with a practical and crisp understanding of the work of a steward and how that work is accomplished. A good steward must not bury his talent. Instead, he has a fiduciary duty to produce for his or her leader.

A good steward is much like a caring and trustworthy gardener who lovingly and faithfully cares for his employer's garden as if it were his own. To produce a harvest, the good steward maintains a watchful eye and works consistently in the vineyard that Jesus entrusted his leader with. The goal of the good steward is to gather the harvest. What is needed is a thorough understanding of the purpose coupled with a willingness to follow the mission defined by the vision of the set leader. Focus and faithfulness of the good steward allows the harvest to grow and achieve mission success. Yet, accountability is two-fold. For meaningful and enriching management, the good steward must be responsive; focused; and helpful to the work assigned. In like manner, the set leader also has an obligation to provide qualified oversight as well as meaningful and enriching management. His or her actions must bring the body of Christ into deeper revelation, instill greater biblical insight, and open the hearts of believers to receive Christ. It is mandatory that the church's administrative plan be rooted and grounded biblically.

Untapped Resources

As management theory has grown over the years it has left an indelible footprint on the day-to-day workings of corporations, service industries, governmental agencies, and the like. Still, far too many ministries appear to have been left behind mainly because some have neglected, were unable, or out-right refused to evolve with modern practices, strategies, and methods of management. The result has been catastrophic primarily for smaller ministries that often lack the resources, support, and many times even the mentorship of larger organizations. Still, there are also those ministries that have fallen behind because of poor management along with a myriad of other reasons. Today, it is seemingly less and less uncommon to read or hear of ministries that have experienced mismanagement, confusion, splits, and gross negligence within their organization.

Sensibility demands that we not take administration lightly. Take into account the "many well known, deemed spiritually responsible, and highly regarded" leaders who are under investigation for impropriety and even face criminal charges as a result. There are untapped resources within most ministry organizations. These are often highly skilled people, some of whom have received *bona fide* training from accredited institutions, work sources, *etc*. Yet, like sleeper agents, they remain idle and inactive members until something goes awry. The Scripture warns us that an idle mind is the devil's workshop. It is beneficial to put these qualified members to work. Teach them, if need be, to get on board. Allowing apt members to fruitlessly observe is a type of resource ministry waste. It is imperative to get everyone involved.

In 2 Thessalonians 3:9–11, the discouraged apostle Paul led by example against idleness, saying to the Thessalonians, "[It was] not because we do not have a right [to such support], but [we wished] to make ourselves an example for you to follow. For while we were yet with you, we gave you this rule and charge: If anyone will not work, neither let him eat. Indeed, we hear that some among you are disorderly [that they are passing their lives in idleness, neglectful of duty], being busy with other people's affairs instead of their own and doing no work."

Sadly, idleness opens the door to gossip, premature judgment, and rash insinuations that can cause new-comers to lose trust and confidence in the church. Left unchecked, this behavior may create eruptions and/or morph into more complex issues that can produce negativity and schisms in the ministry. The apostle Paul spoke strongly against disruptions and disturbances that have wounded, maimed, and destroyed the faith of others. Romans 13:10 reminds us that, "Love does no wrong to one's neighbor [it never hurts anybody]. Therefore love meets all the requirements and is the fulfilling of the Law." When we love God, we are unable to sit idly by on the sidelines. A church founded on the biblical principles of management, filled with the Holy Spirit, and teaching sound theology will motivate members to action.

> Know that the Lord, he is God; It is he who has made us, and not
> we ourselves;[a] We are his people and the sheep of his pasture.
> —Psalm 100:3 (NIV)

Believers in Christ are one body of many individual members. Christ goes on to say through the writings of the apostle Paul in 1 Corinthians the twelfth chapter, "And, God hath set some in the church, first apostles, secondarily prophets, thirdly teachers, after that miracles, then gifts of healings, helps, governments, diversities of tongues. Are all apostles? Are all prophets? Are all teachers? Are all workers of miracles? Have all the gifts of healing? Do all speak with tongues or interpret?" (1 Corinthians 12:28–30).

What this Scripture brings to light is that, though we are one body that does not mean we are all to take the same action. Each member of the body of Christ has his or her own part or use within the body. Romans 12:4–5 clearly reveals that every believer has a specific role or assignment to do within the church. Let's go deeper.

Get the Right People in the Right Place

> Before I formed you in the womb I knew [and] approved of you [as My chosen instrument], and before you were born I separated and set you apart, consecrating you; [and] I appointed you as a prophet to the nations.
>
> —Jeremiah 1:5

It is not ability, righteousness, or depth of knowledge that promotes a man to a position—it is God. So don't oppose or argue with the pastor and leaders within the ministry for not selecting you for the job, and certainly:

> Don't raise your fist against High God. Don't raise your voice against the Rock of Ages. He's the One from east to west; from desert to mountains, he's the One. God rules: he brings this one down to his knees, pulls that one up on her feet. God has a cup in his hand, a bowl of wine, full to the brim. He draws from it and pours; it's drained to the dregs. Earth's wicked ones drink it all, drink it down to the last bitter drop!
>
> **(Psalm 75:6-8 MSG)**

The amplified translation puts it this way:

> Lift not up your [aggressive] horn on high, speak not with a stiff neck and insolent arrogance. For not from the east nor from the west nor from the south come promotion and lifting up. But

God is the Judge! He puts down one and lifts up another. For in the hand of the Lord there is a cup [of his wrath], and the wine foams and is red, well mixed; and he pours out from it, and all the wicked of the earth must drain it and drink its dregs.

—Psalm 75:5–8

The Lord is seeking those who will worship him. Promotion is frequently a byproduct of faithfulness unto the Lord and the mission of God. Even when our labor seems to be unappreciated, we are obligated to be good stewards. The disciples endured much hardship for the sake of the Gospel, "To this hour we have gone both hungry and thirsty; we [habitually] wear but one undergarment [and shiver in the cold]; we are roughly knocked about and wander around homeless. And we still toil unto weariness [for our living], working hard with our own hands. When men revile us [[b] wound us with an accursed sting], we bless them. When we are persecuted, we take it patiently and endure it. When we are slandered and defamed, we [try to] answer softly and bring comfort. We have been made and are now the rubbish and filth of the world [the off-scouring of all things, the scum of the earth]" (1 Corinthians 4:11–13).

The Greek term *steward*, according to Number 3623 in *Strong's Exhaustive Concordance of the Bible* is defined: ἐπίιττροπος and οἰκονόμος transliterated: oikonomos; (phonetic pronunciation: oy-kon-om'-os).

> Root: from G3624 οἶος - transliterated: oikos (phonetic pronunciation: oy'-kos, and from the base of G3551 νόμος transliterated: nomos (phonetic pronunciation: nom'-os); a house-distributer (i.e. manager), or overseer, i.e. an employer in that capacity; by extension a fiscal *agent* (*treasurer*); figurative a preacher (of the Gospel): - chamberlain, governor, steward.

A good steward cannot do his own thing because he do not like or agree with the thing he or she is being asked to do.

> Let every person be loyally subject to the governing (civil) authorities. For there is no authority except from God [by his permission, his sanction], and those that exist do so by God's appointment. Therefore he who resists and sets himself up

against the authorities resists what God has appointed and arranged [in divine order]. And those who resist will bring down judgment upon themselves [receiving the penalty due them]. For civil authorities are not a terror to [people of] good conduct, but to [those of] bad behavior. Would you have no dread of him who is in authority? Then do what is right and you will receive his approval and commendation. For he is God's servant for your good. But if you do wrong, [you should dread him and] be afraid, for he does not bear and wear the sword for nothing. He is God's servant to execute his wrath (punishment, vengeance) on the wrongdoer. Therefore one must be subject, not only to avoid God's wrath and escape punishment, but also as a matter of principle and for the sake of conscience.

—Romans 13:1–5 (AB)

Not everyone is called to be a leader, but whatever the call—and especially those who manage the work—leaders have a duty to be found faithful, consistent, and diligent to the ministry. Whether a leader or a member, it's important to put your money where your mouth is to support the work. However, being on staff does not mean that you should always be at the table. Would you barge into the White House or force your way into the president's office demanding an audience? How much more, then, are we to respect the office of the man or woman of God?

Principled leaders understand the need for protocol. They are competent and unafraid of standing tall while submitting to the set leader. Being submitted does not diminish who you are. It takes wisdom and training to know when, where, and how to interact with leadership and the body of Christ at large. This is a valuable attribute that far too few people possess. Well-seasoned leaders are committed to the mission and the vision of the pastor because they love the set leader, the mission, and believe in the vision.

Tapping into Divine Purpose

Shrewd pastors watch for the quintessential persons within their ranks who display the three fundamental principles: faithfulness, accountability, and effectiveness. Like corporations, the church needs a way to evaluate the performance of its staff regardless of whether they are volunteers or paid workers. Take corporations for example. They tend to try to keep those employees whose performance evaluations exceed or at least meet the company's expectations. These employers do not typically falsify staff evaluations with undeserved flattery. In fact, most companies are finding that constructive criticism is an aid in helping employees continue to progress on the job. I am grateful for the leadership who has cared enough to provide me with critical feedback on my performance. Their constructive criticism has proven beneficial. After employing their feedback, the result has been increased responsibility, wages, and overall job satisfaction. Constructive criticism that is received in a positive manner and put into practice can empower a person to develop and grow. Proverbs 26:28 says, "A lying tongue hateth those that are afflicted by it; and a flattering mouth worketh ruin."

Flowery evaluations are empty and designed to make someone feel good about him- or herself, but this flattery does a disservice to the individual being evaluated and discredits the entire concept. Conversely, constructive criticism enables people to improve. In order for this process to work the evaluator must effectively communicate the cons and the pros.

Benefit comes through effective communication. It opens the way for objectives to be implemented, and that sponsors progress. In businesses, employees whose performance evaluations are high typically receive compensation through pay increases, promotions, bonuses, and the like. Their performances are to aid in determining whether an individual is what is commonly called a "good fit" for the company.

CHAPTER 4

Setting it in Motion

Communication can be likened unto a game of Ping-Pong: either it will be rhythmic and flowing or wild and out of control. Effective communication must be at the core of the management of ministry. When multiple parties are involved, information can become foggy or get lost in translation.

Write down a statement, then gather ten people. Place them in a circle, whisper the statement into the ear of the person next to you, and have that individual do the same into the ear of the person next to him. Continue on to the last person. When the statement reaches the last person have her say out loud what she heard. Lastly, read aloud the written statement and notice how far from what was written the statement has become.

Miscommunication can lead the hearers off course and cause the integrity of the mission to be doubted. The key to ensuring sound management and productivity is transparency. Both transparency and truthfulness are essential elements that must be applied to set protocols and strategies. People like to know that what they have been told is accurate. When events, dates, and times are marketed do all that is possible to keep those set days and times.

Other key factors in managing ministry are protocols and strategies. They work together to help create what is commonly known within many businesses and corporations as *information management*. Information is an important aspect of managing and maintaining reliability, which is a key element of ministry control. The process of controlling information ensures the success of the operation, and it is accomplished by incorporating policies and procedures. Creating and developing predefined, useable processes is the *modus operandi* of this ministry administrative assurance plan.

Staff is able to more easily comply with management decisions when applicable policies, procedures, and processes have been outlined. Further, the use of pre-orchestrated standards will increase the levels of accuracy and uniformity of those following the mission of the organization. One result is the insurance of ease in distributing communication within and without the body of Christ. The driver is the management of information (the written procedures, policies, and processes), the vehicle is the staff. The staff utilizes the information in place to conduct activities, circulate, and disseminate determinations of management. In other words, a ministry administrative assurance plan is essential to the success of the mission because it provides tangible direction for activities, control for competent communication to internal and external members and outreach. It helps leaders circulate and disseminate information.

There must be storing, tracking, and monitoring information. An ample management plan with a focal-point on theology in its practice is needed. However, it is much easier to find a comprehensive theory on management that focuses on individual tasks or narrowly focused principles. During my search there were not many manuals on church management. There were many books on a more secularly based administrative solution than those defined specifically for ministry management.

Faith-based organizations require a comprehensive administrative concept that is founded upon biblical principles. The goal is to authenticate the needs of the church and ministry through a concrete plan that offers godly solutions to sophisticated issues. Accomplishing this task calls for God-driven information, which stems only from Scripture. The church needs a tactically sound management strategy based upon God's Word. This cannot be derived from secularly focused books. More secularly based books lack the main characteristic for ministry management—divine insight. Therefore, the end result of using a more secularly based concept is the failure to conceptualize. All too often, ministries adhering to administrative programs that are not biblically based become more polarized. They often develop splits and fractions (cliques) within and without the body because some leave in rebellion.

I have served in the area of administration for over three decades, working both within the church, corporations, and as a consultant for independent business owners. My goal is to offer godly solutions to help ministries manage real problems that can overwhelm leadership and dissuade members. This book is not intended to be a fix all, but the methodology behind this work stems from a systematic scriptural perspective. There is a greater work published by the renowned scholar R. Alec Mackenzie. He first published his paradigm exploring solutions for real church problems in the November-December 1969 issue of *Harvard Business Review*. MAAP also endeavors to solve genuine ministry issues by uniting modern administrative practices with theological methodology.

As a young woman my parents often reminded me, "In order to know where you are going, you need to know where you have been." Knowing implies an intimate knowledge. It is more than being a bit familiar. The same is true in relation to administration. A lack of knowledge and understanding can cause disconnects and create near-miss situations or complete failure of the projects at hand. There are more organizations that believe they have a firm grasp on administration than actually do. Believing something is true does not make it a fact. Administrative management is too vital to a ministry's success to rely on guessing. We must know.

One aspect of administration is that it is not something that is set in stone, stagnant, or unmoving. Instead, a more precise definition would be fluid and evolving. The answers lie within its inherent nature. The dynamic of administration is productivity. Information constantly changes, so it is necessary to keep up with the process of change. Think about the process taken to complete a project twenty years ago. The steps used then would probably be insufficient for even the exact same assignment today. What is the problem? Strategy! The nature and the makeup of things change, as do the stratagem of administration. Look below at some of the New Testament renderings regarding the godly function of administration. Godly administration is:

1. The practical outflow that meets needs and gives thanks to God (2 Corinthians 9:12–15)
2. The act of being guiltless in stewardship by helping others in faith to God (Titus 1:5–9)
3. Striving to be approved by God (2 Timothy 2:15)

4. The practice of what you believe; putting faith into action (James 2:14–18)

5. Acknowledging/accepting God made us "one" with varied gifts (1 Corinthians 12:18–28)

6. Keeping your eye on the goal which is to imitate Christ (Philippians 3:13–17)

7. Setting order (1 Corinthians 14:40)

8. Not harming others in Christ through our freedom (1 Corinthians 8:7–13)

9. Devotion to the apostles' doctrine and fellowship (Acts 2:42)

10. Disciplined (Romans 15:14; Colossians 3:16)

11. Restorative (Galatians 6:1)

12. Turns the heart of a sinner and backslider to God (James 5:19–20; Matthew 18:15–18)

The list above is not exhaustive, yet even with this limited list it can be seen that there are a number of Scriptures impressing upon the reader the magnitude of a godly administration. Every role has applicable value from a biblical perspective. It is relevant for leadership to be intimately aware of the far-reaching effects of the ministry of administration.

Attempting to focus on all areas within Scripture that lead us to establish an administrative foundation can be an overwhelming task. As a result, we will focus our attention on the four areas I've personally found through experience to be of immense value:

1. Purpose
2. People
3. Planning
4. Providence

Planning causes us to ask ourselves how we will deliver. In order to appropriately answer this question, a ministry management plan (MMP) must be developed. Each of the elements listed above is needed in the development of a comprehensive administrative system. To truly satisfy ministry affairs, implementing one and leaving out the other is insufficient and a recipe for failure. For example, what value is purpose without people working the vision? Similarly, what are the benefits of idle people who are not working in the ministry to bring about its mission?

As previously stated, this work is not a fix-all. However, in order to gain the maximum benefit we will slightly delve into the operation of tasks. Let us begin by trying to conceptualize and construct a plan for managing. MAAP is the groundwork or a type of substratum for ministries to employ a practicable application that is meaningful and able to bull's-eye the targeted objective.

As with most biblical things, there are preconditions:

Planning

God is the Creator of all things. His plan begins with disclosure. He makes known his plan by revealing himself. His plan is not lacking. He sheds insight on the obstacle that has determined to fight in opposition to his plan. (Genesis 3:15) Regardless to the battle waged against him, his plan is thorough.

God unfolds the power and the method of his plan by showing us the three distinct persons of the Godhead. There is the almighty God, Abba, whom Abraham saw. There is also the Word made flesh who dwelt among us and whom John spoke about. He who is God's only Son, and he sanctified and justified us through his own blood. And, last but not by any means least, the Holy Spirit, who is our Comforter. He guides us and dwells within us.

The Scripture says, "Also I heard the voice of the Lord, saying, Whom shall I send, and who will go for Us? Then said I, Here am I; send me" (Isaiah 6:8).

> Declaring the end from the beginning, and from ancient times the things that are not yet done, saying, My counsel shall stand, and I will do all my pleasure: Calling a ravenous bird from the east, the man that executeth My counsel from a far country: yea, I have spoken it, I will also bring it to pass; I have purposed it, I will also do it."
> —Ephesians 46:10–11

> Who verily was foreordained before the foundation of the world, but was manifest in these last times for you.
> —1 Peter 1:20

Which in other ages was not made known unto the sons of men, as it is now revealed unto his holy apostles and prophets by the Spirit; That the Gentiles should be fellow heirs, and of the same body, and partakers of his promise in Christ by the gospel: Whereof I was made a minister, according to the gift of the grace of God given unto me by the effectual working of his power. Unto me, who am less than the least of all saints, is this grace given, that I should preach among the Gentiles the unsearchable riches of Christ; And to make all men see what is the fellowship of the mystery, which from the beginning of the world hath been hid in God, who created all things by Jesus Christ: To the intent that now unto the principalities and powers in heavenly places might be known by the church the manifold wisdom of God, According to the eternal purpose which he purposed in Christ Jesus our Lord.

—Ephesians 3:5–11

According as he hath chosen us in him before the foundation of the world, that we should be holy and without blame before him in love: Having predestined us unto the adoption of children by Jesus Christ to himself, according to the good pleasure of his will. To the praise of the glory of his grace, wherein he hath made us accepted in the beloved. In whom we have redemption through his blood, the forgiveness of sins, according to the riches of his grace; Wherein he hath abounded toward us in all wisdom and prudence; Having made known unto us the mystery of his will, according to his good pleasure which he hath purposed in himself: That in the dispensation of the fullness of times he might gather together in one all things in Christ, both which are in heaven, and which are on earth; In whom also we have obtained an inheritance, being predestinated according to the purpose of him who worketh all things after the counsel of his own will.

—Ephesians 1:4–11

"That in the ages to come he might shew the exceeding riches of his grace in his kindness toward us through Christ Jesus.

—Ephesians 2:7

Now, watch God's plan in action through three distinct activities. The same Godhead is the one true and living God. In his headship, he orchestrated the plan of creation and redemption (1 Chronicles 29:11; 1 Corinthians 3:23; 11:3). In his veritableness, he, the Son of God, is good and true. In utter obedience, he chose to lay down his own life and allowed himself to be separated from his Father to die a horrendous death that destroyed death, sickness, and disease forever (John 1:3; Ephesians 3:9; Colossians 1:15–18; Hebrews 1:1–3; 1 Peter 2:24). And, he who is sweet, honest and all powerful, the Holy Spirit, executed the plan of the Father as given by the Son. In measure, he fills every born-again believer. Yet, believers who ask to be baptized are filled with dunamai (might, ability, and power) to perform great exploits for the Father in Jesus' name (Genesis 1:2; Job 33:4; Luke 1:35; John 3:5; 14:16–17, 26; 16:7–15; 2 Peter 1:21).

The Lord shows us the power of planning to ready the ministry to act. Yet, planning is not a small feat. There are various types of planning that must take place if the ministry is to evolve and ascertain its goals. To involve itself and develop activities designed to serve others, it may be worth the investment to have a dedicated person, a planning coordinator, to manage progress, maintain schedules, and to organize affairs and activities so missions can be realized. It is insufficient at best to assume that a calendar with all the events listed on it constitutes a plan. Many churches attempt to use the church secretary to track annual events, but this can be an overwhelming responsibility and certainly one that the set leader does not have time to manage. The bottom line, poor planning emits poor results. In other words, fail to plan, plan to fail. As timing can be a friend or foe, the allotment of proper preparation time for an event can be crucial to its success and ultimately the ministry as a whole.

Planning Modules

Plan of Action Report (PAR)

A major ingredient to successful planning is the development of a monthly plan of action report (PAR). Use the monthly report to create and develop meeting agendas. This will make weekly or biweekly PAR meetings more meaningful and efficient. Getting an early handle on long-lead action items (those activities that will take the most time to achieve) is important. This step may help prevent missing deadlines especially those that can become blurred or forgotten with the passing of time. In purchasing, long-lead items are things that can take up to six months to arrive. In ministry, on the other hand, long-lead actions may take years to complete. Investigatory research will provide a rough idea of the length of time needed to appropriately plan.

Short Term Planning

As stated, a good employment of PARs is to use them to initiate agendas because agendas formed from a well-organized action plans will help to eliminate time-waste, forgetting key points, missing the small details, and encourage greater participation. The end result will be far more productive and inviting. For intense meetings or long sessions, plan in a short break. Distribute materials such as handouts, notes, charts, *etc.* Encourage sharing; a person may have experience in an area they are not responsible for that can provide valuable assistance to others.

Another essential element in planning involves describing how something will be accomplished within a certain timeframe. Charts and diagrams are great tools for this. Visual aids help people remember. They can also be captivating. Be creative; introduce interesting stories, cartoons, and other mediums surrounding the topic.

More often than not, past experiences provide key information that can be useful for future planning. There are all sorts of tools such as forms, charts, diagrams, reports, checklist, *etc.*, that can be of tremendous value. Have your team keep the dates, handouts, and other pertinent data in a binder. Remember to purge and replace the old information as needed. A cluttered, disorganized binder is of little to no use.

Work Breakdown Schedule (WBS)

The work is typically broken down into parts. This work breakdown schedule (WBS) allows the effort to be defined in measureable stages with specific objectives. Documenting allows the ministry to capture and capitalize on accurate and helpful data.

The planning module includes

- a breakdown of the work to identify what you plan to achieve via creating a detailed schedule of the plan;
- the development of short-term planning guides of the overall objective;
- utilization of tools like charts and diagrams, and checklists for progress reporting;
- development of PARs, including one that envelopes preparation for the rough spots (identifying potential hazards);
- conduct performance evaluations using written records to quality assure (QA) the effectiveness of each staff whether volunteer or hired and provide critical feedback to enhance the strengths of the staff evaluated—focus on their *strengths*.

Planned goals, whether they are short- or long term, are the foundation to build upon. They offer a tactical thought aimed at an idea. The methodology is to structuralize the activities for the mission beforehand. Executing the plan requires the utilization of the 'Ministry of administration' which is using God's plan.

Purpose

Effective management calls us to commit to organizing the administrative structure in accord with God's plan without diluting or diverging from the written text. For the administration to be biblically adhesive, the concepts and methods of integrating the Word of God is paramount. Purpose is the rationale; it satisfies the reason for the event which should give glory unto God. Purpose is a motive for lives to be transformed because it not only gives direction and focus, it also feeds or answers the individual's question, and that allows change. Thereby, confidence and power are released and the individual becomes capable of taking the appropriate action. Thus, purpose is a driver that backs up the leader's position with reasoning and relevancy.

People

Ministry leaders are known by multiple names including staff, officers, followers, gifts, and stakeholders. Since a stakeholder is a bit of an unusual term in ministry, let me define it. Stakeholders are people with an interest or concern in the ministry that reflects God's choice. They are individuals who are in covenant relationships with God and the ministry.

Regardless of the name chosen for leaders within the ministry, they should derive from those identified in Ephesians 4:11, whom God called gifts for the body. They are easily identifiable because they are required to mirror the Word of God. In Ephesians, these gifts are referred to as the five-fold and are godly resources designed specifically by the Lord to perfect the church until we all come into the unity of the faith.

The gifts revealed in Ephesians are not assigned by man. Neither the set leader nor anyone else can call or assign any person to these offices. They are "callings" from God to ministry. Therefore, only the Sovereign Lord can call a man or woman to one or all of these offices. The God-instituted process of ministry cannot be measured in the immense value that it provides to the church, and to the community in which it is called to serve.

Human Factoring

In corporations, human factoring offers a number of reliable strategies such as risk management analysis and health and safety aspects of people and the environment. It is a key component in the field of health, safety, and environmental services (HSSE). Ministry can also make use of some of the aspects of human factoring. Ministries require an effective way to deliver. Believers are commanded by God to take dominion over the earth. Therein, ministry has an obligation to make a positive influence on people and the environment. How can this happen? One way is to think ahead on programs that the ministry can implement that will make an impact on people's health and safety through learned godly behavior. It is through the function of staffing that missions are able to be realized. With proper staffing the ministry is able to conduct its affairs, complete its assignments, help the community, and reach out globally while simultaneously equipping the ministry. To do so, there is need for a genuine method of determining whether the right people are in the right place and moving in the right direction.

A good way to know if there is proper alignment is to infuse the ministry with the consistent practice of directing and evaluating. In order to assess performance, the set leader or designate must first have predefined job descriptions that reflect responsibilities, the time needed to accomplish assigned tasks, and allow for priorities, interruptions, or the redefinition of tasks that could occur. They should think or look futuristically at ways to build respect, collaborate, encourage optimism, and keep morale high.

Assessing staff can be a means of deriving high morale. Assessing people gives individuals the opportunity to reveal their capabilities. The purpose of assessing is to determine the person's abilities in relation to their specific assignment along with their ability to meet deadlines. A good by-product of authentic evaluations is building character. During this process, it is imperative that the evaluator remain focused on the strengths of the person being assessed. If reorganization of tasks is necessary, let it be based upon finding strengths uncovered during the evaluation process.

For example, determine what information needs to be obtained in the evaluation. How do you get the information that you are looking for to draw an accurate understanding? There are many kinds of assessments that deliver different types of analysis. Three pertinent methods of obtaining assessment information are quantitative, qualitative, and peer assessments. The quantitative portion of the assessment will tell you how much was done. A sample would be if ten tasks were required to be accomplished for the year and five were completed, the quantitative analysis would show half the work was done.

It is not enough to get a quantitative analysis without a qualitative analysis. The qualitative analysis gains helpful insight on the details that tell why the five tasks remained incomplete.

Lastly, the use of peer assessments can potentially be of potent value. However, this should be well thought out and carefully planned before implementing. It is wise to have peer assessments shared in love and based upon biblical principle. For example, anonymous exchange of information about the performance of a peer has no place in the ministry. Anonymous exchanges are nothing more than one-sided views that can become filled with innuendo and flawed information. This approach is scripturally unacceptable. The use of an assessment form could be a good way to conduct peer assessments.

Sample of a Type of Peer Assessment Form:

Place the number from 1–10 in the column that best fits your opinion. Choose only one answer.	Strongly Agree	Agree	Average	Strongly Disagree	Disagree
Criterion A					
Criterion B					
Criterion C					
Criterion D					
Criterion E					
Criterion F					

Not all will agree with assessing jobs within the ministry. There may be arguments that classify it as worldly and useless. The short answer is to check the root of their argument; where one argument is being raised; there is an opposite to the argument that also exists. That means, if there is wet there is also dry, if there is good there is also bad, if there is happy there is also sad. The fact remains that evaluations can bring meaningful results that people will not always like or feel flattered by. Yet, as believers in Christ, we are duty-bound to edify the body of Christ and bring glory to God through our works. In order to know if we are in keeping with the command to do good works, the technique of evaluating is a powerful tool when it is done the Lord's way.

Since for every cause there is an effect, the evaluation raises a decision factor. In essence, everything causes a domino effect of whether to retain, reposition, or release the individual. The key to positive assessing is application. Assessing officers using the right method can produce wanted returns. A form should be created that clarifies performance expectations. The form should identify the key factors of the mission along with the related tasks of

- purpose
- process

- principles
- payoff
- approach

In the evaluation, be particular and not general. Remember the evaluation is for the person in front of you whose name is written on the form. You are seeking detailed information regarding his or her performance. Be diligent in discussing each subject to gain specific, accurate responses. All staff should be rewarded for their sincere efforts regardless of the degree of success.

Providence

Providence can be defined as the protective care of God. Our destiny is guided and sustained by the power of God. Meaning, providence is divine, it is God. Our part is to wisely manage what he has bestowed upon us. In order to perform our tasks faithfully and diligently, integration of Scripture with current, relevant administrative practices must be the principle platform used. More simply put, God's principles must be the basis for all policy.

CHAPTER 5

The Modus Operandi (MO)

The approach is to present intention to ministry through objectives in order to lay out a scope of work via a roadmap that utilizes concept-driven administrative practices that deliver. The detailed activities that stem from the use of these applications are designed to enable the development of a structural core. Another very important part of the approach is to prepare work instructions and a project execution plan (PEP). Work instructions are detailed processes designed to provide specific, step-by-step job details. The ministry's PEP is a high-level list of the overall tactical processes, plans, and strategies designed to assist in implementing the delivery.

The PEP is a tracking tool that can serve as an at-a-glance guide for better manageability and preparation for handling changes within ministry business affairs, large or small. These affairs can include removing or replacing assets, purchasing items, or major supplies needed for a special event. In addition, the PEP is effective as a handout in meetings and keeps leaders in the loop on what to expect, anticipate, and plan for. The use of a PEP can minimize distractions, help to manage conflicts in information, and provide a review of details for specific planned missions.

Equipping is a verb always used with an object. It is the furnishing or supplying of an individual's needs to set them up or outfit them—be it emotionally, intellectually, or spiritually—with the resources they require. The purpose of equipping is to ready the ministry for change. Equipping helps to prepare for tasks that lie ahead, especially considering these tasks will probably fluctuate, causing more change.

Conflict, Change, and Conviction

The insignia of change is conflict, and the collision of conflict can thrust a person into change. Life is filled with conflicts. Still, most people do not embrace change. Change often moves one's life into the unknown or the unfamiliar. A company goes bankrupt, forcing a person to find a new job. An illness causes an individual to have to accept early retirement. The death of a loved one brings certain changes to a spouse's life.

Change will break one man apart while another, under those same conditions, will emerge as a leader. How we handle change is important because it gives life new meaning. Change is fluid and evolving, so there must be something that remains constant. For a genuine leader the constant is conviction. The dynamics of a leader's conviction will have a direct impact upon his or her mission.

Change, because a person's life can be thrown or driven into it, creates a caveat that demands answers. This warning will push a person to question how, when, what, who, and why a thing did or did not happen. Interestingly, it is the questions that fuel direction regardless of the answer. Many times, the answer is already known and the question is a tool used to facilitate the answer. Having the answer leads to transformation and becomes the focal point that provides momentum. New focus can propel a leader to fight through the most difficult of circumstances, especially those that threaten their stability or the existence of their assignment.

Questions allow a leader to define or redefine him- or herself and respond with a clear, concise, and organized vision for the mission. Clarity of purpose releases and empowers a ministry to become effective in the community and accomplish its assignment. In addition, clarity helps to protect the authenticity of the leader and closes the door to untimely mistakes that could prematurely abort the mission.

Constructing Collaborators

The metropolis of New Spain in America was divided into Old and New Mexico. It was formerly known as the Empire of Mexico. Old Mexico was situated between New Mexico on the north, the Gulf of Mexico north-east, solid land on the south-east, and the Pacific Ocean on the south-west side.

New Mexico included California which was situated between unknown lands on the north and Old Mexico east.

Montezuma, who met Hernán or Hernándo Cortés who came to invade the land, thought he was the god of his prophecies. Cortés was born in Medellin Estremadura, Spain in 1485. In 1511, Cortés accompanied Governor Diego Velázquez in an expedition to Cuba. Then, on February 19, 1519, with eleven vessels, 508 soldiers and captains, 100 seamen including pilots and masters, sixteen horses, ten bronze guns, four falconets, and thirteen shotguns, Cortés was given charge of a major expedition. In an effort to shake off the authority of Velázquez, Cortés set out to conquer the territory and decided to destroy all means of turning back to Cuba. Yet, not all of the men within his regiment were in agreement. In fact, some were loyal to Cuba. Legend has it that they conspired to seize ships to mutiny back to Cuba, but Cortés moved swiftly into action, ordering all of his men to run them aground or what is better known as "burn the ships." Without the ships the men had no way to return to Cuba, leaving only one choice in front of them: fight or die. They became resolute in their fight against the Aztecs. And so it is with the Christian in his or her journey with the Lord, there is no turning back!

In Luke 9:62, "Jesus said unto him, 'No man, having put his hand to the plow and looking back, is fit for the Kingdom of God.'" Jesus uses leaders who are sold-out. Ministry needs collaborators who are resolute in their commitment to the ministry.

A collaborator is a resource who works jointly on an assignment. In other words, they are the people who "get on board." Collaborators may have the wherewithal, but must also have the aptitude and willingness to serve. Customarily, a lack of understanding hinders a person from getting on board. Miscommunication has led to misunderstandings that destroyed relationships and resulted in assignments that otherwise may have been successful being prematurely aborted.

Oftentimes, communication issues surround the lack of a viable process in place, which can be a major deterrent. The success of a ministry depends largely on its ability to develop faithfulness within its ranks. People are seldom faithful to what they do not understand, cannot identify with, or feel no sense of connection to. Yet, faithfulness is crucial. It ties to accountability. When members become accountable to ministry, productivity and replication are inevitable. Accountability occurs more naturally once plans, processes, and job descriptions are detailed, and assessments are employed.

Framing is needed. It is the framework that holds up the process. Not only is the framework significant, but bear in mind that what is achievable is what was foreseeable. The mind plays an astronomical role in our outcome. Winning, like losing, begins with a thought. A man can lose before ever beginning if he cannot see himself ascertaining what he wants to accomplish. First, get a clear picture of what you are trying to do and then set some goals. The goals should match what has been written in the vision. Now, you are ready to develop a plan of action.

Planning a strategy is an effective way to generate measurable steps toward the outcome. A significant approach to assuring success of the mission is to create policies and procedures. Both are fundamental elements of a clear path forward. With policies and procedures in place, the leader is better able to facilitate the required resources because it is much easier to organize and prepare a budget for events, facilities, utilities, *etc.* Procedures and policies identify what, who, or how much you need to meet the goal. Ambiguity can be a deal breaker for many followers, so having a plan will help get these stakeholders and collaborators engaged in the mission.

An effective leader is able to inspire followers whether they are in total agreement or opposed to the leader's plan. The truth is, people do not always agree with their leader. A good leader is able to coach others and induce them to stay focused and performing at their best to bring about mission accomplishment.

What is germane to strong followers is the mission statement because the mission statement provides the content that sets the tempo and removes uncertainty, mysticism, and skepticism. The mission statement replaces the vagueness with a comprehensible course that defines exactly where the leader is headed. Imagine a pitch black room. Then see yourself running through the room to get to the other side. Would you do it? Can I take a guess and say probably not? Neither would most people. The unwillingness or lack of enthusiasm to run across a dark room stems from the idea of being vulnerable. Why? The problem is vision. Unless a person is blind or vision impaired, most people have an innate need to *see* what is in front of them. Due to the inability to see, whether a person is accustomed to having sight or not, they may feel overwhelmed by the guessing of running through a totally dark room.

The practice of estimating or inciting a trend is the technique of planning, sometimes called *forecasting*. It provides a look-ahead designed to take away second guessing. And it removes the need to generate a new vision, which mainly occurs when the vision is unknown or not understood. Vision empowers the leader to build on the faith of the people, increase their passion, stir hope, and encourage assimilation.

People are needed for the vision to work. So, the knowledgeable leader recognizes the seriousness and priority of appointing qualified resources. And they realize the necessity of being fair-minded and honest in the treatment of each member regardless of whether the services of the staff are volunteer-based or paid. Once selected, it becomes essential to provide training, especially orientation. Training helps with understanding the strategy to tackle the task at hand. A challenge for many ministries is finding suitable volunteers who are called, willing, and able to lead, which further proves training to be a worthwhile investment. In addition, training draws others who are eager to learn and grow with a mission-minded ministry.

Yet, as with most things, there are pitfalls. For example, there seems to be a rise in lawsuits against the church. Thus, there is a greater need to learn and adhere to some modern techniques regarding governing ministries. A good example is the children's ministry. There is no prudence is assuming that a member can be trusted to work with children because they attend services regularly. It is more practical and far-sighted to research an applicable program to guide in appropriately managing a children's ministry. Good ministry programs aid in developing a structure that helps to protect children and defend them against would-be predators.

Scripture reminds us that Jesus is returning soon and to be on guard of the thief who comes in the night, "For you yourselves know perfectly well that the day of the [return of the] Lord will come [as unexpectedly and suddenly] as a thief in the night. When people are saying, all is well and secure, and, there is peace and safety, then in a moment unforeseen destruction (ruin and death) will come upon them as suddenly as labor pains come upon a woman with child; and they shall by no means escape, for there will be no escape. But you are not in [given up to the power of] darkness, brethren, for that day to overtake you by surprise like a thief. For you are all sons of light and sons of the day; we do not belong either to the night or to darkness. Accordingly then, let us not sleep, as the rest do, but let us keep wide awake (alert, watchful, cautious, and on our guard) and let us be sober (calm, collected, and circumspect)" (1 Thessalonians 5:2–6 AB). Know who works in the ministry from the pulpit, the office, the kitchen, to the back door. The Master placed emphasis on *who* he called into service and so should we!

There are biblical principles that reveal God's perspective and selection criteria in relation to staffing his church.

Called: in the Old Testament, Abraham, Moses, Jacob, and even Gideon had supernatural experiences. Abraham was called out of his homeland and promised that his seed would not be able to be counted. Moses experienced God miraculously through a burning bush. Jacob wrestled with an angel who was God in deity form. Gideon received his answer from God via a fleece.

Skilled: others were selected because of their cunning skill. In the book of Leviticus, God chose Bezalel and Oholiab to build the tabernacle because of their superior craftsmanship.

Trained: after Moses led the children of God out of Egypt and was nearing the end of his journey, Joshua was chosen by the Lord to take Moses' place. First, Joshua had to be trained by Moses on how to lead the nation of Israel. Moses' job was to bring the people of God out of bondage while Joshua was tasked with bringing them into the Promised Land.

Obedient: King Saul lost his rule through continuous disobedience. The prophet Samuel anointed David while he was still a shepherd boy to one day take over the national leadership in Saul's stead.

Faithful: Daniel, as a boy, was captured into slavery and selected by the king (along with two other boys) to serve in the palace. The king ordered that the boys should be fed royal food, but they refused the food that would have defiled them and placed their faith in God.

God often chooses those whom we overlook. God looks at the heart while man, like the king, tends to put weight on the outward appearance. When God calls us, the job is a joy that brings fulfillment. He is responsible for making provision for whatever he has instructed us to do. However, when a man calls himself the road is full of pain, sorrow, and ends in utter disappointment and failure. Howbeit, being chosen in and of itself is not enough. The beloved apostle Paul instructed Timothy in 2 Timothy 1:6, "Wherefore I put thee in remembrance that thou stir up the gift of God, which is in thee." Stirring up the gift within you is not just for Timothy, everyone called by God is required to ready themselves for service unto the Lord. He is watching over the gift that he has given to his body to see to it that his people develop their gift by receiving adequate training in order to be ready for the work that comes with the calling.

In Genesis, when God created the earth, he gave us a breadth in view of the layout of his plan. From the first day to the seventh day the most high God of all creation operated in perfect planning. On day one, he said, "Let there be light; and there was light…And the evening and the morning were the first day" (Genesis 1:3–5). On day two, "God said, Let there be a firmament in the midst of the waters, and let it divide the waters from the waters which were under the firmament from the waters which were above the firmament: and it was so…And the evening and the morning were the second day" (Genesis 1:6–8). On the day three, "God said, Let the waters under the heaven be gathered together unto one place, and let the dry land appear: and it was so. And God called the dry land Earth; and the gathering together of the waters called he Seas: and God saw that it was good. And God said, Let the earth bring forth grass, the herb yielding seed, and the fruit tree yielding fruit after his kind, whose seed is in itself, upon the earth: and it was so…And the evening and the morning were the third day" (Genesis 1:9–13). On day four, "God said, Let there be lights in the firmament of the heaven to divide the day from the night; and let them be for signs, and for seasons, and for days, and years: And let them be for lights in the firmament of the heaven to give light upon the earth: and it was so. And God made two great lights; the greater light to rule the day, and the lesser light to rule the night: he made the stars also. And God set them in the firmament of the heaven to give light upon the earth, And to rule over the day and over the night, and to divide the light from the darkness: and God saw that it was good. And the evening and the morning were the fourth day" (Genesis 1:14–19). On day five, "God said, Let the waters bring forth abundantly the moving creature that hath life, and fowl that may fly above the earth in the open firmament of heaven. And God created great whales, and every living creature that moveth, which the waters brought forth abundantly, after their kind, and every winged fowl after his kind: and God saw that it was good. And God blessed them, saying, Be fruitful, and multiply…And the evening and the morning were the fifth day" (Genesis 1:20–23). On day six, "God said, Let the earth bring forth the living creature after his kind, cattle, and creeping thing, and beast of the earth after his kind: and it was so. And God made the beast of the earth after his kind, and cattle after their kind, and everything that creepeth upon the earth after his kind: and God saw that it was good. And God said, Let us make man in our image, after our likeness: and let them have dominion over the fish of the sea, and over the fowl of the air, and over the cattle, and over all the earth, and over every creeping thing that creepeth upon the earth. So God created man in his own image, in the image of God created he him; male and female created he them. And God blessed them, and God said unto them, Be fruitful, and multiply, and replenish the earth, and subdue it: and have dominion... And the evening and the morning were the sixth day" (Genesis 1:24–31). The Lord even included a day of rest in his plan! (Genesis 2:1–3), "Thus the heavens and the earth were finished, and all the host of them. And on the seventh day God ended his work which he had made; and he rested." This pattern of divine order demonstrating meticulous preparation on the part of the Lord, makes absolute the necessity of planning.

We continue to walk with him through Scripture after Scripture while he unfolds his pre-orchestrated plans. We observe the Master's plan of preservation as we watch Noah in obedience and total submission to God. In preparation for a flood that had never before occurred, Noah acquires the materials to build the Ark at God's behest. Next, we witness the almighty God revealing to us his plan to make Abraham the father of many nations. But it does not stop with Abraham. The Bible, in book after book, shows how the almighty God sets plans in motion like pieces in a Chess game. He determines our future. Romans 9:15–21, "For he saith to Moses, I will have mercy on whom I will have mercy, and I will have compassion on whom I will have compassion. So then it is not of him that willeth, nor of him that runneth, but of God that sheweth mercy. For the scripture saith unto Pharaoh, Even for this same purpose have I raised thee up, that I might shew my power in thee, and that my name might be declared throughout all the earth. Therefore hath he mercy on whom he will have mercy, and whom he will he hardeneth. Thou wilt say then unto me, Why doth he yet find fault? For who hath resisted his will? Nay but, O man, who art thou that repliest against God? Shall the thing formed say to him that formed it, Why hast thou made me thus? Hath not the potter power over the clay, of the same lump to make one vessel unto honour, and another unto dishonour?" It is he who orchestrates our lives and futures according to his own design, after his own will.

In the gospel of Luke, the physician presents Jesus to us as a planner. Notice, in chapters 9, 13, 17, and 18, time after time Christ is demonstrated as one who "sets his face to go" here and there. He is not whimsical or irrational. Instead, he is methodical and strategic. With precision and cunning, Christ makes a tactical move. First, he is here and the crowds are chasing after him, some are trying to kill him. Then suddenly, he is gone! How did he vanish? he had a plan. Watch him move in Luke 4:29–31, "And all they in the synagogue, when they heard these things, were filled with wrath, and rose up, and thrust him out of the city, and led him unto the brow of the hill whereon their city was built, that they might cast him down headlong. But he passing through the midst of them went his way, and came down to Capernaum, a city of Galilee, and taught them on the sabbath days."

Again we see Jesus strategically going from place to place to deliver his message, "And it came to pass, when the time was come that he should be received up, he steadfastly set his face to go to Jerusalem, and sent messengers before his face: and they went, and entered into a village of the Samaritans to make ready for him…And he went through the cities and villages, teaching, and journeying toward Jerusalem" (Luke 9:51–13:22).

The ultimate journey of Christ was on Golgotha's Hill, yet we learn through careful observance of his plans as he moved through many places along the way. He told us, "For which of you, intending to build a tower, sitteth not down first, and counteth the cost, whether he have sufficient to finish it? Lest haply, after he hath laid the foundation, and is not able to finish it, all that behold it begin to mock him, Saying, This man began to build, and was not able to finish" (Luke 14:28–30). Thus, we know that a wise man or woman must count the cost or, in today's vernacular, plan things before starting them.

Careful planning can make a huge difference in ministry decisions, which can enable us to become fruitful. Yet, another significant aspect that cannot be overlooked is the magnitude of coupling planning with prayer. For, without prayer even the best planning is of little good. *You must pray!* Pair preparation with prayer and the results will be tangible proof of its phenomenal value. The bottom line is that there is no substitute for seeking God's face to know his will and his way.

The work of the amazing Holy Spirit is to lead and guide us to all truth.

Our job is to ask him for his guidance. Matthew 7:7, "Ask, and it shall be given you." In addition, the Bible says, "In all thy ways acknowledge him and he shall direct thy path." (Proverbs 3:6 KJV) Who is "thy"? It is you. In all of your ways, you are to acknowledge God. When you acknowledge, you admit and accept that he is the one who shall direct the way that you should go.

One of my favorite Scriptures is Proverbs 3:6. In the Masoretic text it says, "There are many devices in a man's heart nevertheless the counsel of the Lord that shall stand." Nothing can stop God. Regardless of the circumstances or the issues, it is powerless to stop God. The key is to remember to always seek God's solution so that your way is governed by the Lord!

A Visible Presence

It is important for the set leader to make his or her presence felt through visibility. Oversight is assuring. It is in no way the same thing as micromanaging. Oversight is the action of administrating the work to ensure unequivocal success in handling of the processes. There must be a supervisor and a subordinate. The word subordinate is not an ugly term when it is understood. A subordinate is a recognizable "contributor." The role of contributor is a win-win arrangement. Both the ministry and the one being supervised are challenged and stretched to grow. The challenge faced by the supervisor is how to deal with directing the temperament of each resource or follower.

The act of supervising is a complex intercommunicative role that must meet the needs and desires of each individual. Some ministries call the person responsible for overseeing a work the director. Their function involves the control of the operation. The work of the director is the management or conduction of the affairs to regulate matters according to ministry standards. These standards serve better when they are organized and written and not made up as one goes along.

Someone must facilitate the activities, handle conflicts, motivate, coordinate, delegate, and manage change. When there is more than one person involved in anything there is bound to be conflict. Name any organization with more than one person working that has not run into some sort of conflict that needed to be resolved. Change alone brings conflict.

Babies born into the world are hopefully not motionless. To get newborns to move or to take their first breaths doctors will stimulate babies by tickling or plucking the bottom of their feet. Like the newborn that responds to the doctor's touch, change too is moving and responsive. According to 2 Corinthians 5:17–21, "Therefore if any man be in Christ, he is a new creature: old things are passed away; behold, all things are become new. And all things are of God." In this text, God speaks of spiritual transformation that takes place at new birth. Yet maintaining an identity in Christ is a daily, continuous, and a life-long process of dying each day to self. But dying is not all. After death has occurred there must be a renewing and a continuous refilling of the Holy Spirit. God's ways and thoughts are not like our ways or thoughts. The Lord is a God of order, for without order what remains is disorder—chaos.

What is obvious in 1 Corinthians 14:40 is Christ's command for us to do things decently and in order. The Lord who is our Savior is not a God of confusion, he is Jehovah-Shalom, the God of peace and wholeness. His desire is that we learn to mirror Jesus Christ, the God of order. Governing the ministry using organized and pre-structured methodology brings order and helps individuals become aligned with ministry concepts, structure, and purpose. Aligning ourselves with the ministry is the act of obeying God and getting onboard with what God has purposed. Obedience is not a choice or a sign of weakness, it is a requirement for every believer in Christ. Obedience is an outward display of willingness and the decision to connect with Jesus in his death, burial, and resurrection.

The book of Genesis is a fantastic book filled with insightful demonstrations of divine delegation. In chapter after chapter, God discloses the weightiness of delegating as he continuously delegates his chosen servants to perform tasks according to his set plan.

Adam, in the Garden of Eden, was commanded to care for it. Abraham delegated his steward with the duty of finding his son, Isaac, a wife. Isaac's son Jacob had a son named Joseph who was delegated by God to save the nation of Israel before they ever became a nation. Joseph's journey started with a seemingly misunderstood dream that landed him in a pit and took him to a prison. Divine providence stepped in and brought him to the palace of pharaoh, and it was in the palace that his ultimate mission and the revelation of God's plan began to unfold. Using the wisdom of God, Joseph coordinated the resources of Egypt to preserve his family, who became a mighty nation.

The act of delegating is a central theme throughout the Bible, as is rightly judging. Being able to rightly judge is a critical facet of ministry. It is vital to ministry success to be able to determine the scope of the people within the ministry. Knowing the culture enables the set leader to put the right people in the right places. Proper oversight will help the leader get the right people in place to plan and work the ministry.

Central to organizing resources is utilizing applicable tools such as org charts and diagrams. These tools are designed to provide clarity in order to enable mission readiness and success. They also provide transparency of the authorities and systems that leadership has appointed.

Job descriptions are another instrumental tool designed to provide a step-by-step or at least a clear path for the individual to follow. First, a job description tells the person what is expected of them within the position. Second, it identifies the qualifications necessary to do the job. Third, it lays out preset boundaries by outlining the specific responsibilities and the role of the job. The institution of providing a job description began with the Lord. In Exodus and Leviticus the Lord gave detailed job descriptions to the priests. Failure to comply with the Almighty's job description was an irreversible termination. The Lord did not allow do-overs. Nor did he leave the priests to guess about his directives. They knew exactly how to perform their duties. They were provided with step-by-step job descriptions. The Lord gave explicit details of what he required and of their tasks, even for the garments they were to wear, the objects to be placed in the tabernacle, when and how to come before him, down to how to get priests out of the Holy of Holies if they were killed for improperly coming into his holy presence.

Today, due to a lack of discretion and fidelity, there are religious organizations whose ethical issues and improprieties have left them with legal battles and soiled names. Some almost overlooked Scriptures in the Bible are Proverbs 22:1a, "A good name is rather to be chosen than great riches," and in Ecclesiastes 7:1, "A good name is better than precious ointment; and the day of death than the day of one's birth."

So many have fallen for improprieties including improper use of public donations, using ministry grants and funding for private or personal use, unethical business practices, illegal activities, and more.

The above list is by no means exhaustive. Rather, it is a small sample of the traps that far too many believers have fallen into. The Bible plainly warns us to beware, "immorality (sexual vice) and all impurity [[a]of lustful, rich, wasteful living] or greediness must not even be named among you, as is fitting and proper among saints (God's consecrated people)" (Ephesians 5:3 AB). Shun the very appearance of wrong doing so that we are not guilty of hindering anyone from desiring to know Christ due to impropriety.

Biblical Principles for Profitability in Business

For ministry to triumph, the right people must be in the right places! So, instead of selecting people solely on the basis of their ability to handle money or because they are related to us, appoint the person who is known for their honesty, whose veracity is substantiated by a proven track record and undeniably strong moral conduct. Yes, ministry does require capable people who can handle budgets, purchases, and varied types of finance, but they must also be godly in conduct.

With obstacles like the ones listed above, how is the ministry to determine who is qualified? Faithfulness to previous assignments is a key determinate of a person's ability to handle ministry finance. The use of written evaluations of previous ministry assignments, similar to the evaluations used by employers, can be evidence providing tangible support to aid in selecting the right fit for the job.

Not only is the use of the individual's past performance of value, judging whether their behavior in relation to their business affairs with others mirror's Christ is also paramount to selecting the individual to the finance committee. In other words, you should be able to see Scriptures like 1Timothy 3:2–7, 12 in the candidate's lifestyle.

God says in Titus 1:7 that those who are considered for position within his church are to "be above reproach." The point is to ensure the soundness of the financial system. This will take planning and organizing job descriptions that clearly outline predefined responsibilities for each person on the financial committee. This action will assist with incorporating oversight into the system for integrity of the system.

In addition to maintaining a strong, healthy committee, it is imperative that the leader not overtax or overburden the committee members. Another benefit of written job responsibilities is pre-assigned tasks. Each staff member is allotted a specific position, thus each is better able to engage in his or her role with a greater degree of success.

Note that the board of directors is a separate administrative entity that has not been written about or defined here. Typically, these members do not and should not serve in the day-to-day operations. They are persons with oversight in the ministry's fiscal affairs. In another important note, the assignment of who serves on the finance committee in the church is a selection that should be made by the pastor, the one to whom God gave the assignment. Heading the committee is the finance director or chairperson. The position of the chairperson is to serve as the business administrator. At times, the chairperson may serve as a tiebreaker within business matters.

The finance committee includes the finance secretary and the treasurer, and each one of these positions is designed to help the church achieve its operational goals. Again, the list provided is not intended to be exhaustive. Rather, it provides a glimpse into the minimum number of positions required for a strong finance committee. Depending upon the size and needs of the organization the following positions may slightly vary. Regardless of the size of the church, all ministries need a suitable finance committee.

Finance committee positions paired with the associated responsibilities:

1. Finance secretary: primary job is accountants receivable. Responsibilities include receiving and recording all the church contributions, managing all the church receipts, making reports of donations, and distributing reports of accounts as required.
2. Treasurer: primary job is accounts payable. Responsibilities include disbursing funds on behalf of the church and making reports of all expenditures.
3. Chairperson: primary job is chief financial officer and business operations, which can double as financial director. Responsibilities include chairing the finance committee. The finance committee needs a vehicle to assist in promoting, collecting, raising funds, and tracking monies for the church. Therefore, the institution of the committee advisory board (CAB) is needed. This committee is made up of various temporary committees appointed by the set leader to lend support to the financial committee:

    a. Counting committee: primary responsibilities include collecting and recording church offerings, donations, fundraising monies, event monies, *etc.* These persons should also travel with the pastor to collect at varied events.

    b. Audit committee: primary responsibilities include focusing on tracking revenue annually by maintaining a report on each program, event, fundraiser, department monies, *etc.* Keep an audit trail of the overall progress of funds for the church at large.

    c. Budget committee: primary responsibilities include presenting fundraising ideas and varied business ventures to maintain focus to keep and not lose sight of the fiscal budget.

C. S. Lewis wrote, "Integrity is doing the right thing, even when no one is watching." God holds his pastor accountable for the management of his church. Thus, a wise leader uses the prudence of God in choosing the right people for the right place within the church.

Knowing the Culture & the System

To be fully aware of the strengths and weaknesses of the ministry we must uncover its influences. To be diligent in building the kingdom of God, utmost in importance, everyone within the ministry must know and fully understand the mission statement. The process of aligning the culture with the ministry's systems is the management of building a strong core, and that aids in steering members toward ministry objectives.

Many business management text books use the term *controlling* to refer to the activities of management. Businesses use the method of controlling to track budgets, inventory, *etc.* In business there are positions like cost controllers, document controllers, and project controls. These positions use systems and forms created to keep accounts, generate reports, and create effective charts for greater control and measurement.

All too often in the ministry, the term control has negative connotations. Some interpret it as being manipulated, pushed around, or even coerced into doing things they do not want to do. *The American Heritage Dictionary of the English Language defines control* as, "To exercise authority or dominating influence over; direct; regulate, also to hold in restraint; to check". In the field of document management, control is essential. In fact, the control of documentation for some jobs, such as offshore work, can mean the difference between life and death for those offshore workers who might quickly need emergency instructions or operating manuals.

Rather than a negative outlook, controlling can be deemed as a way to ensure progress toward accomplishing established goals. In this sense, controlling is simply evaluating. Be sure the ministry is utilizing the gifts who act in harmony with the ministry's mission. It is Christ who has called these gifts, yet they have not all matured and become skilled.

In the context of ministry, evaluating can be defined as the process by which we provide a reason for the manner in which we deal with the resources that God entrusted to us. Evaluating is a process that goes beyond assessing individuals to encompass services, facilities, and the like. Thus, the technique of evaluating requires a procedure to spell out the criteria. The procedure is to outline the structure for critical input and to layout the preplanned documentation required for mission completion. Some forms or documents that may be required are reporting forms, corrective action reports (CAR) to define and determine deviations, and a reward system to motivate faithfulness and encourage those who have been faithful in the discharge of their duties.

Scripture endows us with biblical truths that support the function of assessing. We see that within ministry assessing is an efficient method to get the right people in the right place.

Getting Leaders in Alignment

Three essential principles that must be demonstrated by those in leadership are faithfulness, accountability, and effectiveness.

An example of how corporations track who to fire and who to keep in the company is the employee's performance records. These records have served companies as proven tools to aid in determining if they have the right people in the right places. Performance reviews are also used to promote, determine pay raises, bonuses, along with other perks for high achievers.

Typically, corporations do not invent or fabricate employee evaluations to flatter them into feeling good about their performance. Neither will that practice serve ministries. Proverbs 26:28 says, "A lying tongue hateth those that are afflicted by it; and a flattering mouth worketh ruin." Flowery evaluations are empty. Assessments designed to make someone feel good about him- or herself with false flattery does a disservice to the individual being evaluated and discredits the entire process. Constructive criticism enables the person to improve, and legitimate progress can be realized through the implementation of objectives and open dialog, which is of the utmost importance. In addition to evaluating resources, the culture must be determined. A ministry out of alignment with its culture will most likely be ineffective. Let's consider some examples of ministries misaligned with their cultures.

Scenario 1—Lack of authenticity

The ministry's set leader implements a new program without collaborating with or providing direction to the appointed staff or leaders. People desire to sign up for the program, but there is no one in a position to assist or direct them. Members become frustrated and lose confidence in the staff or leadership, thinking the miscommunication and lack of a system is their fault.

Scenario 2—Lose of valuable resources

New members join with talents they are excited to bring into the fellowship. They sign up to serve, but find that dates and times appointed to meet are not kept. They are unsure of who to ask as there are no org charts or diagrams in place, they ask around the membership only to receive different answers about the same question. Ultimately, they lose hope and become disconnected.

Scenario 3—Mission failure

Members can lose interest, become discouraged, and fall away from the church or organizations that continuously fail to implement its plans. Poor and inept planning can cause ministries to become stagnant and stale from repetitive ideas or ideas that are never executed. Members will likewise lose interest from initiated programs that lack substance, are impractical, or incomplete ideas that lack follow-through.

Thomas Edison said, "Dreams without execution is hallucinations." The church is a living organism designed to be active and productive within the surrounding community.

God's people are to be handled with love and care, and the desire should be to assist them in reaching their God-given talents and callings. The use of fairness in assessing one's ability should be given and paired with constructive criticism and encouragement. Evaluations are to be firm, consistent, and in total compliance with the set policy. To be clear, we know that there is no such thing as a foolproof system. But, godly evaluations can be a sound tool used to get the right people in place to attain the ministry's mission.

CHAPTER 6

Pull the Trigger

True administrative management is the ability to turn creative concepts into productivity. Ministry management is merging assets with a specific assignment. This merger is dependent upon the structural framework, a pattern or way of doing things that can be easily followed. Basically, these are checks and balances. Structuralizing builds into the system a transparency that keeps everyone in the loop.

Consider the results of failing to assimilate. Jesus said that we are to mirror him. "For if any be a hearer of the Word, and not a doer, he is like unto a man beholding his natural face in a glass: For he beholdeth himself, and goeth his way, and straightway forgetteth what manner of man he was" (James 1:23–24). The ministry, the staff in particular, must resemble the set leader who is to follow Christ. Officers who do not become uniform are typically, heady, high-minded, self-absorbed, unfocused, driven by their flesh, and concerned with their own creation over the plan of the ministry. They create an environment that is chaotic and steeped in confusion.

A ministry that forgets or fails to plan will find the leaders operating blindly and making decisions out of their own desire. When people do not know the answer they tend to make them up, and their imaginations often take them far off course. Eliminate the structure and the system and, like a body without a skeleton, it will fall apart. Structure is the bones of the operation. Resources are like the sinew that holds muscles to bones. All the pieces work together to form movement. Without the resources, the ministry will not get off of the ground.

If you choose not to assess the situation or the officers serving and decide not to direct, the outcome will be disorder, disloyalty, and it can leave an open door to a host of other negative issues that can be divisive and unproductive. The worst part is that the mission will most likely go unmet.

To every action there is a process. A process is nothing more than a way of doing things. The way a ministry is managed has a direct impact on not only those who attend or are a part of the ministry but the community. Ministry processes can influence what onlookers think about God, the church, and believers as a whole. A ministry can make a difference in how others view God and his willingness or ability to render help and direction during their time of struggle.

The synergy from the employment of a process can produce a generative effect. This synergy between agents is felt and releases a type of pheromone in the atmosphere that culminates in ministry endurance and replication. The power of synergy is in connection. Each process is dependent upon the other for its validity and meaning. Once the content has been absorbed into the ministry, the effect is cyclical and stimulating.

In Genesis, God put every "seed-bearing" kind within what he created. He commanded Adam and Eve to "be fruitful and multiply." Thus, it is safe to say that the Lord wants us to reproduce. Yet, in the ministry of administration, if there is to be reproduction there must be a continual merging of biblical principle with administrative practice. This does not happen blindly. It is necessary to assess whether a leader is heading in the right direction. The thought here is not of monitoring or surveillance. The intent is to measure and analyze the efficacy of the office. Is he or she fulfilling the duties of his or her post?

Sound management is the ability to pair assets with assignment and yield the expected harvest. The term *asset* is used in this text to refer to both animate and inanimate objects; because, a component of managing effectively is being organized. Organization allows the ministry to flow more easily. It promotes an atmosphere that is less tense. This ease in the environment promotes stability and productivity. Ministry resources are better able to become productive, assimilate, and develop confidence in handling the affairs of the mission. The tangible and intangible profitability of assimilation is soul winning.

When human factoring takes place within the ministry and the community at large, lives become safer, better, and more godly. People will begin to mirror the Lord in their behaviors, lifestyles, and conversations. The most effective ministry embodies the Word of God as the essential part of their behavior inside as well as outside the ministry.

The Drawbridge

While living on the little island of Bermuda, which is surrounded by the North Atlantic Ocean and warmed to a subtropical climate by the Sargasso Sea, I had the pleasure of crossing what was boastfully explained to me as the smallest bridge in the world. There was a small gap between one side of the island and the other that could only be crossed by this tiny little bridge called the Somerset Draw Bridge. This tiny little bridge, which was small enough to walk across, was originally built in the early 1600s and, though rebuilt in the twentieth century, much of the original stonework remains. In like manner, there is a gap between what one believes and exercises, thus a bridge is needed to close the gap.

Theory is absolutely necessary. It enlightens us and provides the rationale for the effort. Still, without the practical application of theory, the result is chaos and unfulfilled ministry goals. Fruitless ministry stems from being disconnected and unaware. To change dynamics to value and equip the ministry, what is needed are both theory and practical application. The bottom line or the end result for any genuine ministry should be kingdom building. The Lord loves his church. And, the church is obligated by Jesus to grow.

Jesus even cursed the fig tree that was unproductive, "And when he (Jesus) saw a fig tree in the way, he came to it, and found nothing thereon, but leaves only, and said unto it, Let no fruit grow on thee henceforward forever. And presently the fig tree withered away" (Matthew 21:19). The church is to be unselfish in showing the agape (Σ'αγαπώ) love of Christ to a lost and dying world.

Jesus is concerned with *how* his body presents love to the world. When the servants of God misuse, abuse, or fail to use the resources that the Lord has provided then he is displeased. The New Testament sheds light on this subject with the parable of the talents. In this parable, God gave each one of his servants' talents. Each servant was to increase the number of talents that he received. The servants were expected to be busy doing the work of the Lord until the Master returned (Matthew 25:14–30). In like manner, the house of the Lord is to be found vigilant in the service of the Master. The church is to complete the duties assigned, including administration. The church is not to be like the careless servant who was derelict in his duties. Rather, God's stewards are required to be like the Hebrew kinsman redeemer, the *go'el*, in the book of Ruth, who was responsible, willing, and able to freely give. Like the go'el, the church is to freely give to others what the Master has entrusted unto the church. There is a responsibility to share with others, whether the talent being shared is spiritual, financial, or of a physical nature.

According to *Vine's Expository Dictionary of Old Testament and New Testament Words*, in Matthew 25, the Greek word used for *talent* is *talanton* (τάλαντον). The original meaning was *a balance*, then *a talent in weight*, hence a sum of money in gold or silver was equivalent to a talent. The Jewish talent contained 3,000 shekels of the sanctuary, e.g., Exodus 30:13 (approximately 114 pounds).

Yet, in the New Testament the talent mentioned in Matthew 18:24 is of the vastness of the sum, 10,000 talents (f2,400,000) indicating the impossibility of man's clearing himself by his own efforts of the guilt which lies upon him before God. The English definition of the word *talent* denoted something weighed. It is a gift or ability. This meaning is taken from the parable of the talents in the book of Matthew. (Matthew 25:14–30). Then 1 Corinthians 12:28 tells us "God hath set some in the church, first apostles, secondarily prophets, thirdly teachers, after that miracles, then gifts of healings, helps, governments, diversities of tongues." Thus, the ultimate or the express purpose of the gifts is the edification and equipping of the church. Why? So, God's church is effective and functions efficiently. The Lord himself has outfitted the church with the gift of administration. In other words, administration is a spiritual gift.

Faithfulness: Not a Request, a Requirement

Scripture lets us know that the Lord will reward those who are found faithful. "Saith unto him, Well done, good and faithful servant; thou has been faithful over a few things, I will make thee ruler over many things: enter thou into the joy of the Lord" (Matthew 25:23). An essential element in our faithfulness is our ability to produce; because, God is a God of increase! We are expected to bring to the Lord an increase on his investment in us.

The Bible says, "To whom much is given much is required." What you must bear in mind is that there are preset boundaries prescribed by the Master that believers are obligated to administrate within. Christians are confined through obedience to Christ by these pre-orchestrated conditions stated within God's Holy Word. Within the church of the Lord, Jesus Christ is to be the center. We are to remain in him and keep him as the central focus within God's set order. Only then will the ministry or organization be able to accomplish and manage the tasks that lie ahead.

Rightly dividing the Word of Truth is not optional, so it is needful for all in leadership to continue in Christian education. The Scripture makes clear that the Christian is to, "Study *and* be eager *and* do your utmost to present yourself to God approved (tested by trial), a workman who has no cause to be ashamed, correctly analyzing *and* accurately dividing [rightly handling and skillfully teaching] the Word of Truth." (2 Timothy 2:15 AB) Thereby, the body of Christ, and especially leadership, will become sharpened and more perfect in their hermeneutical skills. This will allow godly leadership to be rooted and grounded in biblical knowledge and understanding to better govern the ministry in accord with God's plan.

Although the church has a responsibility for being fruitful there are a good number of them that squander precious time on fruitless activities. Far too many spend long, unfruitful hours in committee meetings that exhaust and waste precious time on issues of far less importance than those that benefit families within the community and members of the body.

Temperament theory lets us know that we are all born with strengths and weaknesses called wants and needs. Many lives within the body of Christ have become fragmented due to poor choices or those inflicted on them by others. In light of the needs of God's people, it is easy to see how the waste of one's time can have a negative impact. There are good programs available that are designed to meet the needs of people, but it takes the ministry of management to make them profitable enough to continue in existence.

The Lord's church, his body in which he is the head, is not a corporation, as corporations are not people. His church is the body of Christ, a living and breathing organism that must mobilize to positively affect the earth.

Mobilization is a readiness for emergencies. Therefore, the body has to come together as one working in harmony and agreement.

The Gravity of Connection

An irreplaceable gem within the church is *connection*. In order to enact a far-reaching administration, it is imperative to establish relationships, invest in appropriate materials to train people who are committed, and help others learn the importance of commitment. The dimension of success is tied to relationship.

The graveness of relationship is in the connection which can be likened unto the heart, lungs, and the skeleton of the thorax. The connection is like the Thorax skeleton, the chest which is a cage, is designed to protect the relationship, these principal organs, the heart and the lungs. Life hinges on their connection. The skeletal boundary is hard as it is designed to provide protection like a shield to prevent obstacles from penetrating and severing this vital connection. The heart lies between the two lungs and there is no vacancy of space. The heart and its' roots are all contained behind the sternum and the cartilages of the third, fourth, fifth, sixth, and the seventh rib on the left side. And, in this intimate relationship these two systems are connected to supply the body with necessary oxygen required to sustain the life that God has given you. In this illustration of the skeleton of the thorax safeguarding the relationship between two tender organs, the heart and the lungs, can be seen the power of connection and the importance of relationship. If the heart nearly stops and loses its' beat, the lungs will gasp for air. If the lungs almost collapse for a lack of oxygen, the heart will increase the blood pressure to generate oxygen. One system will collapse for the other to keep the other from dying. Neither the heart nor the lungs can stand without one another. In like manner, God has instituted his plan of intimacy in relationship through connection to give birth to destiny and cause purpose to reach fulfillment. Relationship is the heart of a successful administration. And, it is from the connection in relationship that resources are able to continue to be gained and the kingdom advanced.

During the process of building relationships, a key focus should be missions. In other words, do not lose sight of the "key," which is being mission minded. God's church should be focused on his commandments, which every believer should know and obey. The Great Commission is no different. In fact, it brings priceless value to the church. It is made up of two important elements. Like Joshua, whose job was to bring the nation of Israel into the Promised Land, the church is to bring people into relationship with God. Jesus has already brought salvation to every believer. Thus, it is the job of the church to bring (converts) the people to Jesus.

Another essential element is aiding these new converts in developing a strong spiritual walk. Now it can be seen right away how administration is a spiritual gift that the Lord gave to the church on and for purpose. In short, he deliberately gave the church the ministry of administration so his people would receive spiritual, material, and physical help. When people are helped they are then better capable of glorifying God in and through their lives. For this reason, being highly skilled in a secular craft or even having studied subjects like accounting, economics, or business administration are simply not enough in-and-of themselves. Howbeit, they do add a certain value. But the fact remains that administration is more of a serving gift designed by God to enable, equip, and facilitate his church so that the church will edify and build up the body of Christ. According to Scripture, in ancient biblical times while the disciples traveled preaching the Gospel throughout the world, the elders remained in the local church administering spiritual direction and praying for the people.

In Acts 6:1–3, the apostles appointed godly men of honest rapport to serve the people of God spiritually, emotionally, and physically by holding fast to the Apostles' Doctrine. These men were not just honest, they were full of the Holy Ghost, who empowered them with divine wisdom. So, these elders were "gifted administrators," and their job was to serve the body of Christ effectively and efficiently with willing hearts. These skilled elders not only had the power, they had the will, conservation of mind, and the authority to effectively administrate within the local body or congregation.

In the above text, *Vine's Expository Dictionary of Old Testament and New Testament Words* employs the Greek word *diakonia* (διακονία) which means "to run errands; an attendant, i.e. (A waiter), a servant, etc., figuratively: eleemosynary aid performing in the office and work of a diakonos." A *diakonos* is a deacon, deaconess, minister, teacher, or pastor. They serviced the ministry, providing spiritual ministration. This word *diakonos* is used for domestic duties and for religious and spiritual ministration of apostolic ministry and the service of believers. However, in the context of Acts 6:1 it is not in the same sense as ecclesiastical. *The Revised Version* (RV) uses the word *ministrations* while *The Authorized Version* (AV) chose *administrations*, but both the RV and AV refer to collectively ministering a local church in service to believers.

Today, many churches undervalue the gift of administration and some have no administration at all. As a result, they fail to achieve what God orchestrated and called for within the local community. Most churches seek secularly qualified people who have no spiritual call or conviction to serve in this important office.

Having witnessed some churches appointing volunteers or hiring workers for this office, seldom have I seen any given any true authority to administrate according to 1 Corinthians 14:12 (edifying the body of Christ which is the church, the body of our Lord and Savior, Jesus Christ). But the gift of administration is needed at the onset of any God-ordained ministry. By this, I mean from the early stages of the church. Why? The office of administration bridges the gap between the spiritual and the physical or human element. As a bridge, it is constructed to unify or join together the relationship afore mentioned. In doing so, it builds trust and instills confidence within the Kuruakn (the Lord's house).

CHAPTER 7

Not Taking It Lightly

His intention was the perfecting and the full equipping of the
saints (His consecrated people), [that they should do] the work
of ministering toward building up Christ's body (the church),
[that it might develop] until we all attain oneness in the faith
and in the comprehension of the [full and accurate (Marvin
Vincent, *Word Studies*)] knowledge of the Son of God, that [we
might arrive] at really mature manhood (the completeness
of personality which is nothing less than the standard height
of Christ's own perfection), the measure of the stature of the
fullness of the Christ and the completeness found in him.

—Ephesians 4:12 (AB)

From Ephesians 4:12, straightaway we see that the Father has specific
and particular expectations of those whom he has called into the service
of administration. He has set particular guidelines and standards. He has
informed us through his logos (written word) what those standards are.
In other words, God has set order. The Lord himself has decided what the
conduct and the lifestyles of those serving in administrative management
are to be. The Scripture tells us that they must walk with humility, godliness,
and with a teachable spirit, all of which is needed to accomplish the work
that the Lord has assigned. It is an obligation to care for his people, so the
administrative team must exercise spiritual discipline, faith in God, and
must convey a submitted heart. These leaders are to exemplify a yielded and
committed disposition by walking and displaying continuous faithfulness to

all of the leadership and, foremost, to the set leader and to the people of God as a whole. Due to the lack of theological information and the absence of a Christian view of administration, all too many churches have settled with using a more "worldly" model of administration in lieu of a biblical model.

In fact, there are multiple approaches and a wide variety of models of administration. *The Harvard Business Review* has compiled pertinent business management material and a number of working strategies for years. Some of these strategies can provide helpful information that can be utilized to help the church improve its structure. Deciding on the right model for the ministry, the model should be biblically based to meet the goals of ministry. For example, the Process Movement [of management] is task centered. Being driven by tasks, it can potentially have a rippling negative effect on church administration.

Process Management is concerned with how the job is done, which has merit. However, it is devoid of the Word of God in its framework, which can lead the church into a dichotomy, meaning an atmosphere of cliques. This fissure is the by-product of the absence of God in its plan. In short, in this scenario the church has chosen a secular business model that excludes Scripture, therefore, it cannot fit the ministry the Lord intended.

Consider another prime example, that of fund raising, which is used by many churches. A number of churches like fundraisers because they can be a major asset in helping the church fund missions. Known to be one of the most easily started and quickly built revenue outlets is the sale of raffle tickets. One year, in an attempt to raise some much-needed funds for a special event, it was decided that we would sell raffle tickets. Most people liked the idea and were eager to win something that was worth far more than the few dollars they had paid for the ticket. But when it became time to organize the sale, one of the church leaders stated that she did not believe in fund-raisers and refused to participate. She called it gambling in the church.

The truth is selling raffle tickets was an effective method of raising money quickly. In fact, many businesses use fund-raisers much like the raffle ticket idea to gain funds for charitable organizations, parties, *etc.*

Let me make a disclaimer lest you miss my point, my objective here is not of judgment. Condemning the use of fund-raisers, whether it is selling raffle tickets, baking cakes, selling plates, or some other activity, is *not* the intent. Instead, the idea is to deliberately instigate a conflict to promote questioning and exact reasoning. The question is, "Do you agree that fund-raisers like selling raffle tickets are in line with Scripture? If so, how does the idea parallel with the Word of God? And, are there Bible verses that support the stance? If not, is the leader right in her thinking that we are out of step with Scripture? If she is not right, how could we show the leader at my church who disagreed with our selling raffle-tickets that we were not out of step with the Scripture? Further, did our action hinder someone's faith? Was our behavior like the Process of Movement model—strictly task oriented?

Another one of my favorite Scriptures is Joshua 1:8, "This Book of the Law shall not depart out of your mouth: but thou shalt meditate therein day and night, that thou mayest observe to according to all that is written therein: for then thou shalt make thy way prosperous, and then thou shalt have good success." The *impact point* is whatever creative plan your church decides to use, the key to good success is in keeping the Word of the Lord. The *driving* question should always be, what does God think about our actions? Someone said well, "Before a person will hear a sermon they must first see one." The apostle Paul was unbending in his teachings, for he was insistent that those working within the ministry must have integrity. Remember my disclaimer, the point was not of accusation or judgment. I am not suggesting what kind of fundraiser to choose or that churches stop having them, nor am I saying that they are unscriptural. The idea here is that of logic. The *intent* is to stir conflict to create questioning and reasoning that cause us to ask what God is saying.

In 2 Corinthians 6:1–17 (AB) the apostle Paul was discussing "'Laboring together' [as God's fellow workers] with him then, we beg of you not to receive the grace of God in vain [that merciful kindness by which God exerts his holy influence on souls and turns them to Christ, keeping and strengthening them—do not receive it to no purpose]. For he says, In the time of favor (of an assured welcome) I have listened to and heeded your call, and I have helped you on the day of deliverance (the day of salvation). Behold, now is truly the time for a gracious welcome and acceptance [of you from God]; behold, now is the day of salvation! We put no obstruction in anybody's way [we give no offense in anything], so that no fault may be found and [our] ministry blamed and discredited. But we commend ourselves in every way as [true] servants of God: Through great endurance, in tribulation and suffering, in hardships and privations, in sore straits and calamities,

In beatings, imprisonments, riots, labors, sleepless watching, hunger; By innocence and purity, knowledge and spiritual insight, longsuffering and patience, kindness, in the Holy Spirit, in unfeigned love; By [speaking] the word of truth, in the power of God, with the weapons of righteousness for the right hand [to attack] and for the left hand [to defend]; Amid honor and dishonor; in defaming and evil report and in praise and good report. [We are branded] as deceivers (impostors), and [yet vindicated as] truthful and honest. [We are treated] as unknown and ignored [by the world], and [yet we are] well-known and recognized [by God and his people]; as dying, and yet here we are alive; as chastened by suffering and [yet] not killed; As grieved and mourning, yet [we are] always rejoicing; as poor [ourselves, yet] bestowing riches on many; as having nothing, and [yet in reality] possessing all things. Our mouth is open to you, Corinthians [we are hiding nothing, keeping nothing back], and our heart is expanded wide [for you]! There is no lack of room for you in [our hearts], but you lack room in your own affections [for us]. By way of return then, do this for me—I speak as to children—open wide your hearts also [to us]. Do not be unequally yoked with unbelievers [do not make mismated alliances with them or come under a different yoke with them, inconsistent with your faith]. For what partnership have right living and right standing with God with iniquity and lawlessness? Or how can light have fellowship with darkness? What harmony can there be between Christ and Belial [the devil]? Or what has a believer in common with an unbeliever? What agreement [can there be between] a temple of God and idols? For we are the temple of the living God; even as God said, I will dwell in and with and among them and will walk in and with and among them, and I will be their God, and they shall be My people. So, come out from among [unbelievers], and separate (sever) yourselves from them, says the Lord, and touch not [any] unclean thing; then I will receive you kindly and treat you with favor, And will be a Father unto you, and ye shall be My sons and daughters, saith the Lord Almighty."

Administrative work is supposed to bring the plans and objectives into focus as based on the Word of God. Therefore, administration must be founded and built upon God's Word, then tasks and accomplishments will illuminate the fundamental principles of the organization. Good success is infectious! For good success, the church must make a priority of mandating the use of the Bible in its approach to administration.

Consider that you cannot separate a person's idealism from their behaviors. An individual's proclivities are often driven by that person's realisms. For this reason, it is imperative that ministry leaders have biblical convictions. Conviction reveals a person's core beliefs and values. The conviction of godly servants must be scripturally based if they are to make positive impact upon the church to meet ministry goals. The old adage of "I missed one" is insufficient.

Theology is often seen as institutional, yet, by definition, it is the study of the nature of God and religious belief. It is dubious at best to think that one can conduct administrative duties within ministry that are in contradiction to theological correctness. The integrity of administration can mean the difference between members buying in to the ministry or seeing it as duplicitous and hypocritical. "Let not then your good be evil spoken of: For the kingdom of God is not meat and drink; but righteousness, and peace, and joy in the Holy Ghost. For he that in these things serveth Christ is acceptable to God, and approved of men. Let us therefore follow after the things which make for peace, and things wherewith one may edify another" (Romans 14:16–19).

Even false appearances can foster an environment of derision, division, disloyalty, and distrust. John Albert Broadus, an eighteenth century American Baptist pastor and professor at Southern Baptist Theological Seminary, observed that a pastor's "leadership style communicates his theology, and his or her theology dictates the way he or she leads with people." Ministry that is reliable and steady is at its core united. In Matthew 12:22–28, when the demon-possessed man who was blind and mute was brought to Jesus for to be healed, "all the multitudes were amazed and said, 'Could this be the Son of David?' Now when the Pharisees heard it they said, 'This fellow does not cast out demons except by Beelzebub, the ruler of the demons.' But Jesus knew their thoughts, and said to them: 'Every kingdom divided against itself is brought to desolation, and every city or house divided against itself will not stand. If Satan casts out Satan, he is divided against himself. How then will his kingdom stand? And if I cast out demons by Beelzebub, by whom do your sons cast them out? Therefore they shall be your judges. But if I cast out demons by the Spirit of God, surely the kingdom of God has come upon you.'" The same condition occurs by taking theology into one hand and administrative practice into the other. To cultivate an atmosphere of faith, strength, stability, and oneness, administration must engraft theology. A biblically based administration not only cultivates but it envelopes the atmosphere with a contagion of truth and order. A church divided against its self cannot stand. One reason for this is division which is disharmonious and forces a split, all of which can be brought on by failure to incorporate tenets within administration.

CHAPTER 8

How to Make It All Happen

A question that temperament theorists have been trying to answer for decades is what is relationship? How do relationships interact with or affect destiny? Simply put, relationships are the links, the connectors, or the conduits to achieving your aspirations. Both vertical and horizontal relationships are necessary for your future to be realized.

Relationship

Relationship is the area where many people fail. Oftentimes, past issues, misguided perceptions, lack of understanding, or lack of knowledge, among other things, hinder people from succeeding in the area of connection. Far too many people miss the key, and are therefore burdened with a multiplicity of unsuccessful relationships. Since, connection is the key one cannot have connection without relationship!

In administration, strong understanding of biblical principle is the foundation upon which relationships should be built. One major definition of ministry is the building of the kingdom of God. But how is this done? It is through assisting people to become more like God and helping them to learn how to mirror Christ through his Word. The aim of helping individuals spiritually develop has to be at the core of the ministry's administrative design. In fact, people will become spiritually exhausted when they spend long meaningless time with vain religious laws and rituals that are fruitless and unfulfilling. It is when we are connected that the body can become whole and empowered to become a people who please God.

The gifts that he has ascribed to the church are his work, thus we are to maintain the order in which he has established them. Since the gifts of God were not created by the mind of man, man then has no authority to modify them. The Word of God is the Master's divine plan to bring man back into fellowship with himself. The Bible says that God does not wish for any man to perish by deviating from the truth. And even the smallest details are meaningful to the Lord. This is a message that the church should carry to the world, God has fitly joined each one of us together that we may be one even as he is 'One'. Yet the choice is ours. The Creator does not force relationship or connection on us.

Moses was wise. He followed God's direction explicitly in building the tabernacle. No part of the construction, artistry, furnishings, service, *etc.*, of or within the tabernacle was left undone or overlooked. Each object and every aspect of its structure was meticulously constructed and prepared according to the Lord's command to Moses. We, too, are governed according to his pattern and must consider our ways in each decision at the minutest turn. A major key to our having good success is determined or limited by our ability to last, to endure, to stay the course. The Word of God lets us know that this race is not given to the swift. Meaning, the race is not given to someone because he or she got the job done the quickest. Rather, it is the person who endures, the one who withstands the test, the one who keeps on refusing to quit. The race is won by the individual who decides to make it to the end. In other words, it is a decision that is based solely on choices.

My intent is not to undermine the complexities of a person's struggles. Victory often comes with a price and seldom without a fight. The reality is that no matter what weapon has been created or formed against any child of God, that weapon is powerless to prosper. Therefore, your victory or defeat is not predicated upon what comes up against you. Defeat happens to the person who chooses to give up. Hence, as the tabernacle ceremonies and oblations were the same in the end as in the beginning, so it is with the church.

Scripture says, "So let us seize and hold fast and retain without wavering the hope we cherish and confess and our acknowledgement of it, for he who promised is reliable (sure) and faithful to his word." (Hebrews 10:23 AB) Rather, opt to be faithful to the end. The foundation is already laid and there is no other foundation to be laid! When hanging on the Cross on

Golgatha's hill, Jesus cried out in a loud voice unto the Father, "*Eli, Eli Lama Sabachthani?*" That is to say, "my God, my God, why hast thou forsaken me?" (Matthew 27:46b).

On that day, he did it all! He destroyed death, sin, and all manner of sickness and disease. Having become sin for us so that we do not have to be enslaved to it; Jesus hung there until there was no more blood to run down, and he hung there till the sun refused to shine. He hung there while they gambled over his clothes, mocked, and ridiculed him while his mother, Mary, lay there at his feet watching and listening to her son suffer in utter agony and remarkable pain. Then, in one moving moment, after all his work was finally done, the Lord most high surrendered himself to the will of the Father. Jesus laid down his own life and said to his Father, "It is finished" (John 19:30). So, there are no new methods needed, no new patterns or structures to erect. We need only to abide by what he has so selflessly already laid. The time is coming and is very near when all those Christians who have accepted him will be in the rapture to meet him in the air.

The Bible says, "But I would not have you to be ignorant, brethren, concerning them which are asleep, that ye sorrow not, even as others which have no hope. For, if we believe that Jesus died and rose again, even so them also which sleep in Jesus will God bring with him. For this we say unto you by the Word of the Lord, that we which are alive and remain unto the coming of the Lord shall not prevent them which are asleep. For the Lord himself shall descend from Heaven with a shout, with the voice of the archangel, and with the trump of God: And the dead in Christ shall rise first: Then we which are alive and remain shall be caught up together with them in the clouds, to meet the Lord in the air: and so shall we ever be with the Lord. Wherefore comfort one another with these words" (2 Thessalonians 4:13–18).

The Word of God reminds us, "For the law having a shadow of good things to come, and not the very image of the things, can never with those sacrifices which they offered year by year continually make the comers thereunto perfect. For then would they not have ceased to be offered? Because that the worshippers once purged should have had no more conscience of sins. But in those sacrifices there is a remembrance again made of sins every year. For it is not possible that the blood of bulls and of goats should take away sins. Wherefore when he cometh into the world, he saith, Sacrifice and offering thou wouldest not, but a body hast thou prepared for me: In burnt offerings and sacrifices for sin thou hast had no pleasure. Then said I, Lo, I come (In the volume of the book it is written of me) to do thy will, O God. Above when he said, Sacrifice and offering and burnt offerings and offering for sin thou wouldest not, neither hadst pleasure therein; which are offered by the law; Then said he, Lo, I come to do thy will, that he may establish the second" (Hebrews 10:1–9).

Without any doubt, we need never forget that it was "Neither by the blood of goats and calves, but by his own Blood he entered in once into the Holy Place, having obtained eternal redemption for us" (Hebrews 9:12). For, in that tabernacle not made with hands, Christ sprinkled his own Blood upon the mercy seat, which is before the very throne of God, and in so doing the question of sin is settled forever. Hallelujah and amen!

Death thought it had won. On Friday it began its celebration, gambling, drinking, and partying all night long in anticipation of a victory it believed it had won. But early Sunday morning the Lord returned to proclaim that the keys had been taken, the sting of death was no more, for the great I Am had risen from the dead! Our salvation was not given to Christ. No, he had to buy it. And the cost of salvation was not cheap. Therefore, we must appreciate this precious and beautiful salvation and make use of it in our lives.

John said, "That he (God) wishes above all things that we prosper and be in health even as our soul prospers." So, it is necessary for the believer to know that God created each of us with purpose and there is no power in the earth or beneath it that can prevail against his church. In John 20:17, Jesus told Mary, "Touch me not," for he had not yet ascended to the Father. But in this text let us listen closer so that we can also hear Jesus saying "we must not delay in immediately coming to God," for our faith and obedience must be "now."

Do not cling to what was. Let go of the flesh so that you can receive the Spirit. Jesus had to ascend to the Father to send the Comforter back to us. Mary wanted to touch the Savior whom she loved and adored. She was accustomed, as were the other disciples, to being near Jesus and to ministering to him. But he had to go immediately to the Father in heaven. Then, in Luke 24:39, Jesus told the disciples, "Handle me and see." Because it was on resurrection day, the Savior went up to heaven and presented his Blood at the altar (that tabernacle that was not made with hands) and sprinkled his Blood upon the mercy seat. Jesus, who had formerly said to Mary, "Touch me not," could now say, "Handle me and see." And, the Lord is still calling for us today to touch him and see! Lay hold of Christ and, like Jacob, refuse to let him go.

Herein lay a major thought: how can any man truly come to know the Master and remain disconnected to his brethren in Christ? In other words, how can you love God and hate your brother or your sister? The answer is found in the written Word of God. Search the Scriptures, for in them is life.

Without a doubt, relationships are vital to destiny. Relationships are the umbilical cord to the survival and the fulfillment of the birth of the dreams that God has given you. To have a ministry or church that is driven by purpose, relationships must be valued and maintained. God's arrangement is not symbolic of an island. Instead, it would be better viewed as a village, a place of community and fellowship. Each one within the community is strengthened by the overcoming testimony of the other. My joy is made fuller by your victory. My delight is in the prosperity of my sister and my brother. Witnessing your success encourages me to continue on the journey with an expectation and an anticipation of certain triumph. Individuals disconnected from the body quickly become weak and easily beaten because they lack the testimonies that reveal the power, the mercy, and the faithfulness of God. The disconnected are individuals limited to their environment and what they alone have experienced.

In Summation

How does the church keep people motivated to stay connected? There are a number of motivational theories designed to equip, enlighten, and even inspire a person to action.

Frederick Irving Herzberg, an American psychologist, was highly known for introducing the job enrichment theory. His model, the Motivator-Hygiene theory identified the factors within the work environment that produced job satisfaction and dissatisfaction. He called the job dissatisfaction factors *hygiene* and he named the job satisfaction factors *motivators*. The hygiene factors are derived primarily from discontentment in the workplace, which is directly related to the framework of the job and not to the day-to-day routine. When certain aspects are given, like pay increase, job security, excellent supervision, better working conditions, quality interpersonal relationships on the job, and more status, the employee may not become satisfied, but when these factors are not provided the employee will certainly be dissatisfied.

Motivational factors are chiefly the reasons that an employee is satisfied with a job. This dynamic is directly driven by the content of the job and relates to the real nature of the work being performed. The staff member will not experience job satisfaction when these factors are neglected. On the other hand, productivity and high job satisfaction occur when the employer provides the staff member with motivational factors. The causes of motivation are increased responsibility, advancement, recognition, achievement, a challenge at work, the opportunity to express or to be creative, and the possibility to grow professionally and personally.

Now, consider the prospect of this on ministry. The use of the elements of Herzberg's model within the parameters or the scope of administration can be impactful. Within the church should be the best working conditions, comparable to any fortune 500 company. Human nature is delicate. Romans 8:3, "For what the flesh could not do, in that it was weak through the flesh," let us know that the structure of God's organization must be biblical. More and more Christians are battling their sin nature and are losing. Most times, the Christian is torn between doing what they want and doing what is right. Even the apostle Paul, who once called himself chief of all apostles, said in his flesh dwelled no good thing, "For I know that in me (that is, in my flesh,) dwelleth no good thing: for to will is present with me; but how to perform that which is good I find not. For the good that I would I do not: but the evil which I would not, that I do" (Romans 7:18–19)

The church of God must remember that the people serving are the same people who were once considered sinful and far from fellowship with Christ but are now sanctified by his grace. So the culture within ministry should show biblical compassion to be able to restore the fallen.

Fallen refers to those who, for one reason or another, are out of fellowship with the Lord Jesus Christ. Maybe their relationship was exhausted by the burdens and pressures of life or bad decisions. Whatever the case, when leadership reminds people of their shortcomings and failures or places unrealistic expectations upon the collaborators it breeds the hygiene factor. These irrational working conditions can leave a person wounded, hurt, and discouraged with ministry. Creating an atmosphere of realism rather than fantasy will help keep ministry resources grounded.

Those who are new to ministry or on their first assignments may have a zeal. Passion is a good thing to have in ministry; however, passion alone is not enough. It takes time, training, mentoring, studying, consecrating, and preparing repeatedly to develop the knowledge and wisdom to effectively minister Christ to others. A novice practicing on the congregation can have a negative impact on members and especially visitors. It is important to keep those new to ministry close to the senior leadership. These aspiring leaders should be provided with constructive criticism, understanding, and guidance. To build a strong culture, leadership must remain prayerful, pay careful attention and provide a listening ear, and watchful eye. Couple this with adequate training and mentoring, the outcome will be a healthy culture of people who are secure and confident.

Having a healthy culture will keep these believers in ministry encouraged. Few realize that victories are won most times after long hours, days, weeks, months, and sometimes years of relentlessly fighting through the storms and struggles and facing the weapons formed for your demise. What is left after the battle is the development of Christian character and the sweet prize of having overcome after the heartaches of having suffered through misunderstandings.

In this technological age, people want and expect things right now. Look around the church: the ministry novice is often called today and preaching today. The new convert is saved this morning and teaching before sunset. Change is inevitable. What worked a decade ago is virtually obsolete today. Words that meant one thing before now have a whole new meaning. All change is not necessarily negative, but we know that change is more than probable. It is a contributor that many times brings positive and meaningful purpose into a person's life.

That is not to say that change cannot also be destructive. Change can be as disastrous as a bowling bowl thrust into a china cabinet when it is ineffectively managed. For example, words that often take on new meanings can quickly become ineffective and create communication nightmares. Therefore, a major center of attention should be placed on the practice of effectively communicating in all mediums of communication. In addition, lack of communication can also create an abundance of misunderstanding. Where no exchange of information exists, people tend to fill in the blanks with misinformation, innuendo, and assumptions. A "heads up" approach promotes the development of a successful staff. In so doing, they will learn to anticipate change. Even negative change becomes less impactful on staff accustomed to receiving a heads up.

Communicating information to staff prior to announcing the information to the congregation can motivate the officers and stimulate unity. Yet, taking too long to pass the information to the congregation can create disharmony and distrust within the body. Good communication supports the belief that the ministry is concerned and cares. It gives the appearance that the ministry seriously takes the emotional wellbeing of its members into consideration. When staff believe that their concerns and cares are taken seriously and are considered even during hardships, the outcome of change can still be positive and advantageous to the kingdom of God.

Two key components in shaping good behavior and enforcing right attitudes in staff members of the church are prayer and connection. Leaders have the awesome privilege of praying for those within their care. The Scripture makes clear that the leader is to take seriously his or her charge to care for those in the service of God. With prayer, locked doors become open, barricades are destroyed, systems are reversed, the impossible becomes possible, and the unbelievable becomes reality.

Secondly, oversight and distance allow for variance. Galatians 5:20 states, "It is obvious what kind of life develops out of trying to get your own way all the time: repetitive, loveless, cheap sex; a stinking accumulation of mental and emotional garbage; frenzied and joyless grabs for happiness; trinket gods; magic-show religion; paranoid loneliness; cutthroat competition; all-consuming-yet-never-satisfied wants; a brutal temper; an impotence to love or be loved; divided homes and divided lives; small-minded and lopsided pursuits; the vicious habit of depersonalizing everyone into a rival; uncontrolled and uncontrollable addictions; ugly parodies of community. I could go on. (The message) This isn't the first time I have warned you, you know. If you use your freedom this way, you will not inherit God's kingdom." (Galatians 5:21 MSG)

Promptly addressing distorted issues, behaviors, and attitudes will often halt confusion. When connection is maintained through periodic meetings, such as brief get-togethers like tea or coffee, lunch, *etc.*, connections are easier to evolve. Lasting damage to both the individual and the church can be remedied through constructing relationship, whereas hidden negative attitudes or behaviors fester and canker because they are permitted to grow without exposure. If these behaviors and attitudes go unimpeded, one result is they become practically impossible to unravel. The ulcer goes deeper, becoming buried in unconstructive and often harmful emotions such as feelings of bitterness. The typical consequence is a broken relationship that has become severed, most times permanently.

Of course, there is a triad relationship that should occur between the Holy Spirit, the individual, and the leader wherein each is responsible for doing his part. Great leaders such as Moses, Joshua, Abraham, Isaac, Jacob, Samuel, David, Huldah, Deborah, John, Mary, and Paul, among a host of others all were committed to the ministry and entrusted other believers to their care. Each of these leaders had ample chance to either become frustrated or allow their discontentment and disappointments with ministry to cause them to walk away. But not one of them put their hand to the plow and turned back. Instead, each man and woman, with their weaknesses, made a choice to honor the call of God on their lives knowing that only the Lord himself could release them from their obligation to the call.

When called to lead, no amount of discord, disappointment, or frustration should be enough to undo the commitment to the appointment of leadership. As a leader, you are entrusted by God with the ministry, the hopes, and the dreams of each member. In other words, the Creator has assigned you the responsibility of showing care, concern, exact preparation, and readiness for what he has called them (the gifts to the body) to do.

Since no one knows how long God will keep them under your watchful eye, take care for the time you have been allotted by the Lord. Remember the servant who buried his talent. The training, the welfare, and the investment that you as their leader have provided have a lifelong impact on the beliefs, values, and application of the Word of God in each members lives.

Take heed, remembering that he is coming soon. Besides this, you know what a critical hour this is, how it is high time now for you to wake up out of your sleep and rouse to reality. For salvation, final deliverance, is nearer to us now than when we first believed, adhered to, trusted in, and relied on Christ, the Messiah. Romans 13:11–12 says, "The night is far gone and the day is almost here. Let us then drop (fling away) the works and deeds of darkness and put on the [full] armor of light."

"'Y'varekh'kha Adonai v'yishmerekha. Ya'er Adonai panav eleikha vichunekka. Yissa Adonai panav eleikha v'yasem l'kha shalom."

"May Adonai lift up his face toward you and give you peace. In this way they are to put my name on the people of Israel, so that I will bless them."

—Numbers 6:24–27

GLOSSARY

{C}

Cyclical: occurring in cycles; recurrent.

{D}

Denarii: a silver coin and monetary unit of ancient Rome, first issued in the latter part of the third century B.C.

Drachmas: a unit of weight in ancient Greece.

Diakonia: Greek word that means: to run errands; an attendant, i.e. (a waiter), a servant, *etc.* Figuratively: eleemosynary aid performing in the office and work of a diakonos.

Diakonos: a deacon, deaconess, minister, teacher, or pastor. is used (a) of domestic duties; (b) Of religious and spiritual "ministration" of apostolic ministry or of the service of believers.

{E}

Efficacy: the ability or capacity to produce a desired or intended result or effect; effectiveness.

Eirēnē: peace, peaceable, peaceably, quiet, quietness. Peace (literal or figurative); by implication *prosperity*—one, peace, quietness, rest, set at one again.

Eiro: to join.

Eleemosynary: ancient Greek word that means generous in assistance to the poor (obsolete); a donation, charitable, charity.

{G}

Generative: capable of producing or creating. Having the power or function of <u>generating</u>, originating, producing, or reproducing.

{H}

Helmsman: a person at the helm who steers the ship.

{I}

Integration: an act or instance of combining into an integral whole.

{K}

Kubernesis: derived from the word *kubernao* which means, "to guide" (English Word used in the KJV meaning "to govern"). The word denotes (a) steering, pilotage (b) metaphorically governments or governing.

Kubernao: to guide (English Word used in the KJV meaning "to govern").

Kuruakn: the Lord's house.

{M}

Mismated: to mate or match unsuitably.

MAAP: ministries Administrative Assurance Plan.

{N}

Non-harmonious: discordant; not marked by agreement in feeling, attitude, or action; not in harmony; not in agreement.

{P}

Pheromone: a chemical substance produced and released into the environment by an animal, especially a mammal or an insect, affecting the behavior or physiology of others of its species.

{S}

Spheres: place or environment within which a person or thing exists; a field of activity or operation; to be out of one's professional sphere. A particular social world, stratum society, or walk of life, *i.e.*, his social sphere is small.

Synergy: the interaction or cooperation of two or more organizations, substances, or other agents to produce a combined effect greater than the sum of their separate effects. Cooperative interaction.

{T}

Talanton: Greek word used for *talent*. A talent in weight, hence a sum of money in gold or silver was equivalent to a talent.

Temperament: the genetic inborn part of man, "who I am;" what God gave me at birth.

Notes

Notes

Notes

Notes

Notes

Notes

Notes

Notes